DIE HAND

THE HAND

27

Herausgegeben von / Edited by Bettina Richter

Essay von / by Arne Scheuermann

MUSEUM FÜR GESTALTUNG ZÜRICH
PLAKATSAMMLUNG/POSTER COLLECTION

LARS MÜLLER PUBLISHERS

1 **Cornel Windlin/Gregor Huber**
Schauspielhaus Zürich/Saison 2010/11
2010

VORWORT

Nonverbale Verständigung lebt von Mimik und Gestik. Nicht nur in der Kommunikationswissenschaft, auch in der visuellen Anthropologie, der Psychologie, der Soziologie, der Semiotik und Linguistik bilden Gesicht und Hand einen wichtigen Forschungsgegenstand. In der Plakatgeschichte und so auch im reichen Fundus der Plakatsammlung des Museum für Gestaltung Zürich finden sich unzählige Hand-Variationen, die diese komplexen Bezugsfelder visualisieren. Denn neben dem Gesicht besitzt die Hand die grösste appellative Wirkung. Beispielhaft dafür ist das Bild des Zeigefingers, eine anthropologische Universalie. In der amerikanischen Plakatikone «I Want You for U.S. Army» (James Montgomery Flagg, 1917) richtet sich der Indexfinger von Uncle Sam direkt auf den Betrachter, im Plakatkontext den künftigen Soldaten des Ersten Weltkriegs. Das auf den Finger reduzierte Bildzitat findet sich bis heute in abgewandelter Form auf Plakaten wieder. Im Sinne eines magischen Imperativs wird hier der Standpunkt des Rezipienten vehement eingefordert, Absender und Empfänger begegnen sich im unmittelbaren Dialog.

Kunsthistorische Vorbilder unterschiedlicher Kulturen dienen Plakatgestaltern häufig als Anregung für ihre Handabbildungen: Streng stilisiert, realistisch wiedergegeben oder expressiv überhöht und verfremdet, ist die Hand Gesten- und Symbolträger par excellence. Während das Motiv in der Kunst ab dem 17. Jahrhundert vor allem die Persönlichkeit und damit die Individualität der Porträtierten verdichtet, setzt das Massenmedium Plakat auf die universal verständliche Gebärde und die Allgemeingültigkeit ihres sinnbildhaften Ausdrucks. Am explizitesten zeigt sich dies in Handnegativen oder im Handabdruck, sprechendes Zeichen menschlicher Präsenz schon in der vorgeschichtlichen Höhlenmalerei. Die blosse Zeugenschaft des Abdrucks wird in anderen Plakaten zur konkreten Botschaft, wenn die Handfläche als Projektionsfläche schriftlicher und bildlicher Mitteilungen dient. Als sensibles Werkzeug demonstriert die Hand im Produktplakat den Gebrauch der zum Erwerb angebotenen Güter oder bietet diese dem potenziellen Käufer verführerisch-nahsichtig an. Im Dienst von Politik und Propaganda kommt die konventionalisierte Geste zum Einsatz: Die Schwurhand, das Victory-Zeichen oder die gereckte Faust sind rhetorische Symbole einer kollektiven Bildsprache. Die von oben monumental herabgreifende Hand nimmt gar die Tradition von Michelangelos Erschaffung Adams auf: Die göttliche Übermacht verkehrt sich dabei häufig in den autoritären Anspruch weltlicher Mächte.

Die Hand wird vom Geist geführt, bildet diesen aber auch. Sie ist Instrument sowohl zärtlicher als auch gewalttätiger Handlung und Ausdrucksträger eines breiten emotionalen Vokabulars. Als Zeichen des kreativ schaffenden Menschen beeindrucken aber vor allem auch ihre formale Schönheit und Beweglichkeit. So wird die Hand in Kulturplakaten zur Metapher des Lebens schlechthin.

Bettina Richter

FOREWORD

Gestures and facial expressions underpin all kinds of non-verbal communication. That means that the study of hands and faces forms an important research field not just in communication studies, but also in visual anthropology, psychology, sociology, semiotics and linguistics. Countless hand variants that give visual expression to these complex reference fields run through the history of poster design and are therefore also found in the extensive Poster Collection of the Museum für Gestaltung Zürich. For, alongside the face, the hand has the most forceful appellative impact. Representations of a pointing index finger, an anthropological universal, are one striking example. In the iconic American poster "I Want You for U.S. Army" (James Montgomery Flagg, 1917), Uncle Sam's index finger is pointed straight at viewers; in the poster's original context, at prospective First World War soldiers. The visual quotation still appears in modified form on posters to this day, reduced to nothing more than that finger. Like some magical imperative, it demands forcefully that recipients consider their vantage point, setting up a direct dialogue between the sender of the message and those intended to receive it.

Poster designers often draw inspiration for their depictions of hands from the art history of a whole host of cultures: highly stylized, realistically depicted or expressively heightened and alienated, the hand is the vector par excellence for gestures and symbols. Whereas since the seventeenth century this motif has served in art as a condensed expression of the personality and hence the individuality of the person portrayed, as a mass medium the poster concentrates on universally comprehensible gestures and globally valid symbolic expression. This is revealed most explicitly in outlines or prints of hands, eloquent signs of human presence ever since the days of prehistoric cave paintings. In other posters, the testimony symbolized by the handprint is transformed into a specific message when the palm of the hand becomes a screen onto which written and graphic messages are projected. The active hand is a kind of sentient tool on product advertising posters, demonstrating how to use the goods in question or holding them out to potential purchasers in alluring close-ups. Conventionalized gestures appear in the service of politics and propaganda: the hand raised to swear an oath, the victory sign and the clenched fist are rhetorical symbols of a collective visual language. The monumental hand reaching down from on high even takes up the tradition of Michelangelo's creation of Adam, with the supreme divine power frequently mutating into the authoritarian ambition of worldly powers.

The hand is guided by the spirit, but it also shapes the spirit. It is an instrument of acts of tenderness and violence, and a conduit to express a wide-ranging emotional vocabulary. More than anything else, however, it is the hand's formal beauty and mobility that leaves a lasting impression as a symbol of human creativity. That means that the hand becomes a metaphor of life itself in posters from the cultural realm.

Bettina Richter

2 **anonym**
La pègre au pouvoir
1968

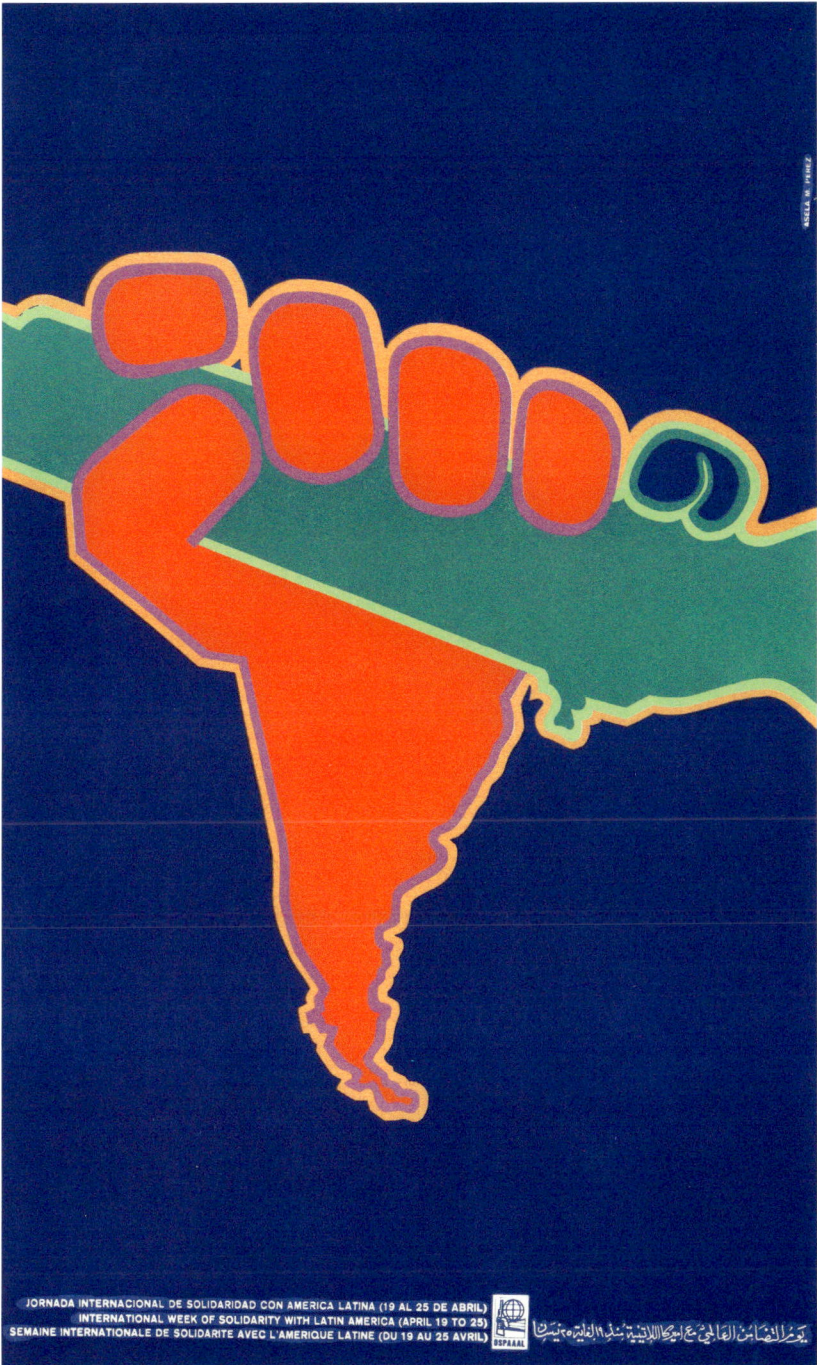

3 **Asela Maria Pérez**
Jornada internacional de solidaridad con America Latina
1968

4 **Ben Faydherbe / Wout De Vringer**
[ohne Text]
2008

5 **Adolphe Mouron Cassandre**
Thomson/La main-d'œuvre électro domestique
1931

6 **Uwe Loesch**
Ich bin Rahmen für Handlung. Ich bin Kunstdruck
für Druckkunst. Ikonolux von Zanders
1986

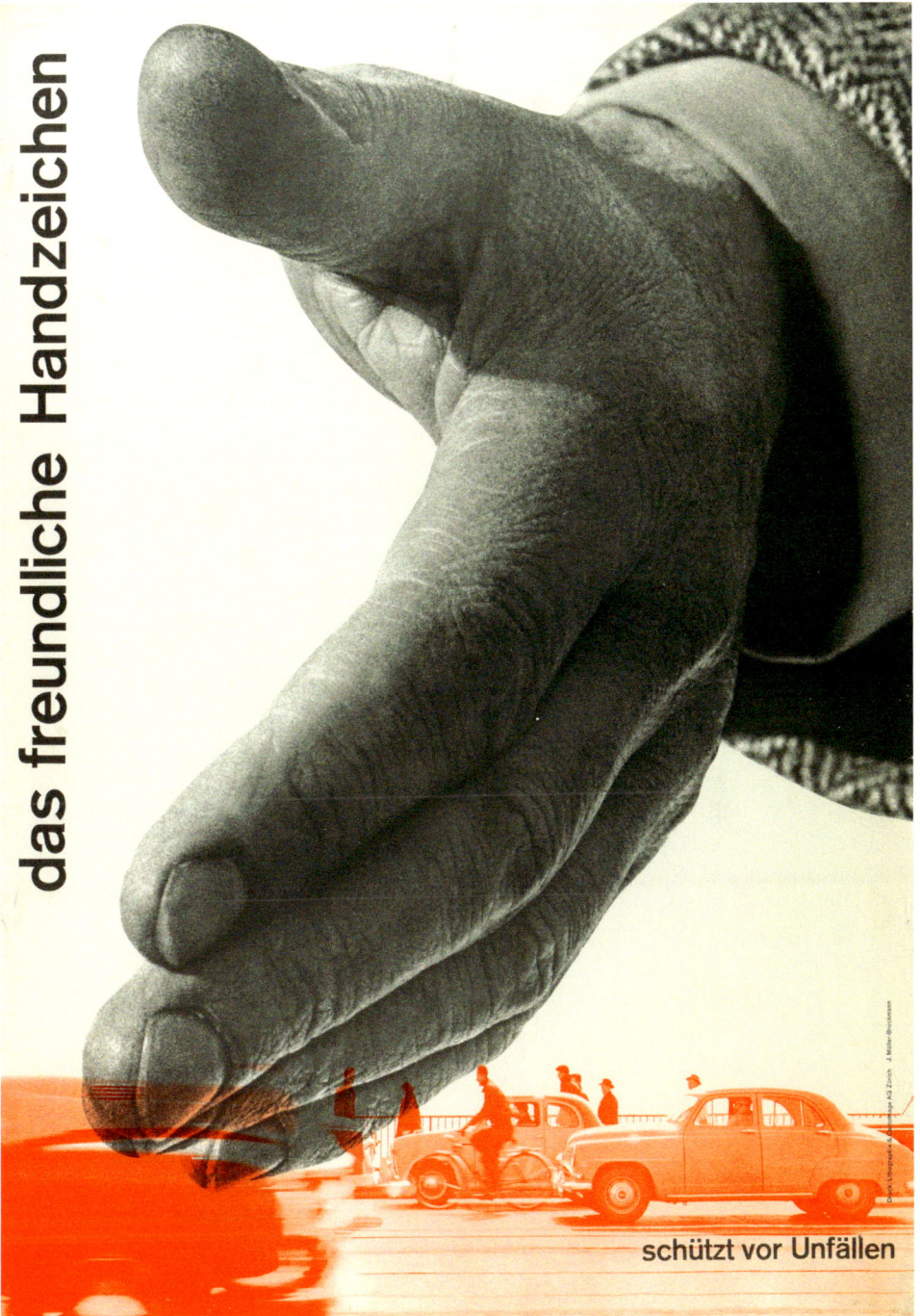

7 **Josef Müller-Brockmann**
Photo: René Burri
Das freundliche Handzeichen schützt vor Unfällen
1955

DAS HANDELNDE PLAKAT –
ZUR VISUELLEN RHETORIK DER HAND AUF DEM WERBEPLAKAT

Arne Scheuermann

HANDMODELS UND MODELLHÄNDE

In der Filmkomödie *You Don't Mess with the Zohan* (USA 2008, Dennis Dugan) flieht der gefeierte israelische Superagent Zohan Dvir frustriert von Krieg und Auseinandersetzungen in seiner Heimat nach New York, um sich seinen wahren Lebenstraum zu erfüllen: eine Karriere als Friseur. Doch aller Anfang ist schwer – und von den ersten Rückschlägen enttäuscht, entschliesst er sich, bei einem Bekannten unterzukommen und im Elektrofachhandel «Going Out of Business» als Verkäufer anzufangen. Doch dessen Besitzer rät ihm davon ab. «Dieser Laden ist ein Killer für Lebensträume», erzählt der Chef, während er den Blick über seine Angestellten schweifen lässt, und er berichtet, was diese eigentlich hatten werden wollen, bevor sie der unerfüllte amerikanische Traum in den Alltag eines Elektroverkäufers zwang: Rennfahrer zum Beispiel oder Comedian. «Yosi wollte Handmodel werden», fährt er trostlos fort – und wir sehen, wie ein gesetzter Mann mit Bart und hoher Stirn einem Kunden mit geschmeidigen, wohlüberlegten Gesten ein Handy präsentiert, indem er es mit der einen Hand entspannt hält und mit der anderen in eleganten Drehungen auf seine Vorzüge deutet, wie man es aus dem Verkaufsfernsehen kennt, wenn etwa Uhren, Messersets oder Staubsauger angeboten werden A. Welche Wendung der Film nehmen wird, ist damit klar. Wenn dieser Laden in der Lage ist, einem Handmodel mit einer derartigen Begabung den Lebenstraum zu zerstören, was geschähe dann erst mit dem Helden und seinem Wunschtraum vom Leben als Friseur?

Den Beruf des Handmodels gibt es wirklich, und sein Erfolg, so lernen wir in dieser kurzen Szene trotz aller parodistischen Übertreibung, ist das Produkt verschiedener Bestandteile: Neben Beharrlichkeit, Begabung und der Chance zum Durchbruch reicht die schöne Hand allein nicht aus, sie muss auch zeigen und anpreisen können B. Sie muss die Gesten beherrschen, dies elegant zu tun. Sie muss all die Schwingbewegungen und Zeigegesten ausführen können, die den Blick lenken und die Ware ins rechte Licht rücken. Was zuallererst eben auch heisst: Die Hand allein verkauft nichts, sie braucht etwas, das sie präsentieren kann. Waren.

Seinen Ursprung mag der Beruf des Handmodels daher auf dem Marktplatz haben – also vor Jahrtausenden schon. «Sehen Sie her – haben Sie schon einmal so einen feinen Stoff in den Händen gehalten?! Kommen Sie! Sehen Sie selbst! Prüfen Sie selbst!» Dabei streicht die Hand des Verkäufers über den Stoff, fasst zärtlich den Saum, zeigt auf das Webmuster, prüft die Festigkeit zwischen Daumen und Mittelfinger – und es ist nicht undenkbar, dass neben dem wortreichen, schlagfertigen Händler auch derjenige einen Vorteil auf dem antiken Marktplatz hatte, der es verstand, mit der Rhetorik schöner Gesten die Waren an den Kunden zu bringen.

Die Hand, die die Ware anpreist, mag demnach so alt sein wie der Handel selbst. Und so verwundert es auch nicht, dass es mit dem Aufkommen des Werbeplakats wie selbstverständlich Hände sind, die die Waren halten, anpreisen, benutzen und darbieten. Mit der Blüte der Werbefotografie sind es dann zunehmend professionelle Handmodels, die die Uhren präsentieren, die Zigarettenpackung halten und auf Waschmittel zeigen. Wobei die Physiognomie der Model-Hand in weltanschaulicher Angemessenheit zur jeweiligen Ware passen muss: kernig männlich der behaarte Rücken der Hand, die den Cognac-Schwenker hält – schlank die Frauenhand, die die Seife zwischen Daumen und Zeigefinger präsentiert.

DER HANDSCHUH MUSS ZUR HAND PASSEN

In der Wissenschaft der Rhetorik übrigens ist dieses Prinzip der Angemessenheit – unter dem Namen *aptum* – ebenfalls zentral. Denn stets müssen Redeform und Gegenstand eng aufeinander abgestimmt sein, wenn die Rede überzeugen soll, stets müssen inhaltliche Höhe der Rede und Affekthöhe der Präsentation zueinander passen, wenn die Rede erfolgreich Gefühle wecken soll. Diese Regelsysteme umfassen seit der Antike nicht nur die Verfertigung der Rede, die Lehre von den rhetorischen Figuren oder die Techniken des Auswendiglernens von Reden, sondern auch das wirksame und affektreiche Halten der Rede selbst. So verwundert es auch nicht, dass die Rhetorik im Laufe der Jahrhunderte ein recht ausgefeiltes System der Gestik entwickelt hat. Denn nicht nur auf dem Marktplatz wird die Ware geprüft, auch vor Gericht oder im Parlament zeigen Redner auf Mitstreiter oder heben anklagend den Zeigefinger. Diese Gestiklehre für Redner wurde dann im Laufe der Zeit, insbesondere ab der Frühen Neuzeit, auch für das Schauspiel, die Predigt und den Bühnengesang angepasst und weiterentwickelt.

Entlang der Konzepte von *natura*, *ars* und *exercitio* – also der Natürlichkeit der Geste, dem kunstfertigen Einsatz derselben und der Übung der Gesten als Grundlage ihrer Beherrschung – wurden auf diesem Wege umfassende, hochspezialisierte Regelbücher für Pastoren, Opernsängerinnen und Theaterschauspieler entwickelt, die bis in kleine Details regeln, bei welchem Redegegenstand die Hand geöffnet zum Himmel zu führen sei, wann die Faust auf das Herz pochen sollte, wann die Handflächen ratlos das Schulterzucken begleiten. Auf alten Zeichnungen und Gemälden sind wir noch heute mit diesen Gesten konfrontiert; einige verstehen wir spontan, als wären es Gesten unserer eigenen Zeit, bei anderen braucht es nicht selten eine kompetente Übersetzung, um zu verstehen, was sie bedeuten sollen. Etliche solcher Hände aus der Kunstgeschichte sehen wir auf dem Plakat «Ich bin Rahmen für Handlung» versammelt, auf dem sie humorvoll allesamt zu Zeigegesten umgedeutet werden 6.

Die Gesten der Schauspieler, Prediger und Sängerinnen wecken nicht nur beim Redner selbst Affekte – ein physiologischer Zusammenhang, den Sie jederzeit im Selbstversuch nachvollziehen können: Versuchen Sie nur einmal, eine Liebeserklärung mit

A

geballten Fäusten zu machen, oder beschimpfen Sie jemanden mit entspannt nach oben weisenden Händen! Auch im Zuschauer und Zuhörer erzeugen die Gesten Ge- -fühle, sie ordnen den Vortrag, betonen und strukturieren den Verlauf der Rede und ermöglichen die Identifikation des Publikums mit dem Dargebotenen.

Das Repertoire hierfür ist gross. Im *Historischen Wörterbuch der Rhetorik* beispiels- weise – der zentralen Übersicht der Rhetorikforschung – wird zusammenfassend zwischen mindestens fünf Arten der Geste unterschieden: den andeutenden Gesten, Gesten der Nachahmung, Ausdrucksgesten, Gesten der Anrede und emphatischen Gesten.[1] Die Gesten des Handmodels etwa wären in dieser Systematik vor allem dem ersten Bereich zuzuordnen. Die Schönheit der Hand und die Wirksamkeit ihrer Zeige- geste stehen dabei im Vordergrund. Die Zeichen, die hierbei zum Einsatz kommen, sind vor allem indexikalische; und das verwundert auch nicht, meint der Begriff Index im Lateinischen doch auch den Zeigefinger. Aber auch Hände auf Plakaten, die keine Waren anpreisen, lassen sich – wie später noch gezeigt wird – als Gesten verstehen und etwa den Ausdrucksgesten und emphatischen Gesten zuordnen.

Dennoch, und damit kommen wir zurück zu den Beispielen, lassen sich nicht alle Hände auf Plakaten allein auf das Konzept der Geste reduzieren, denn viele Hände gestikulie- ren gar nicht, sondern handeln, stellen Zeichen dar oder stehen einfach durch ihre wiedererkennbare universale Form für den Menschen an sich.

HANDELNDE HÄNDE
Damit gerät die zweite Gruppe von Handmotiven in den Blick. Denn neben den Händen, die präsentieren und anpreisen – also jenen Händen, die im eigentlichen Sinne die Funktion des Plakats als Zeigemedium durch nochmaliges Zeigen verdoppeln – gibt es auf den Plakaten dieser Sammlung unter anderem auch solche Hände, die weniger Waren anpreisen als vielmehr Gegenstände benutzen. Mag die Hand, die die Zigarette hält, hier noch einen denkbaren Grenzfall darstellen – andere Hände kreuzen Wahlzet- tel an, stehlen Brieftaschen, ergreifen Hämmer und bedienen Telefone. Hände greifen Essstäbchen und führen den Schreibstift, regeln den Radioempfang und verteilen

A Filmstill aus *You Don't Mess with the Zohan* (USA 2008)

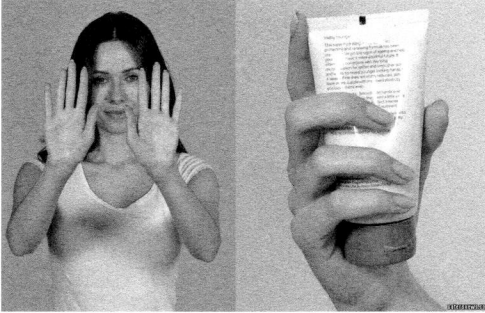
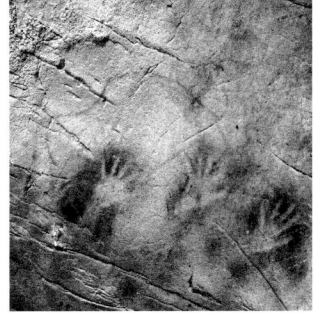

Saatgut. Hierbei erfüllt die Hand unterschiedliche Funktionen, mal ist sie die zupackende Verlängerung des Arms, mal die feinmotorische Basis der Finger.

Und doch tritt die Hand in diesen Darstellungen nicht selten hinter der Bedeutung ihres Tuns zurück: Nicht das Benutzen der Wählscheibe, sondern das Telefonieren ist gemeint. Als visuell-rhetorische Figur der Metonymie steht die Hand dann für die jeweilige Tätigkeit selbst, an der sie beteiligt ist: Es geht um die Wahl, den Taschendiebstahl, das Handwerken, das Essen, das Schreiben, das Radiohören und die Saat.

Die tätige Hand wird damit potenziell auch zur Metapher für die Arbeit ganz allgemein. Die Werktätigen als der mit den Händen schaffende Teil der Bevölkerung werden in der erhobenen Sichel, dem geschwungenen Hammer sichtbar. Die Handlung wird zur Geste. Die Geste wird zum Symbol.

STOP! GO! VIVE LA RÉVOLUTION!
Damit wären wir auch schon bei einer dritten Gruppe von Hand-Topoi angekommen. Diese Handdarstellungen liessen sich grob als sprechende Gesten beschreiben. Sie richten sich direkt an die Betrachter, gerade so, als wäre das Plakat ein lebendiges Gegenüber. Die Hand, die durch die Stopp-Geste Einhalt gebietet, die Hand, die gierig nach Erspartem greift, die Faust, die zur Revolution aufruft, weil sie im Ernstfall auch zuschlagen könnte – in diesen Beispielen formt die Hand ein Zeichen, das als solches erkannt werden will. Hierbei sind die Übergänge zwischen Ausdrucksgesten – wie etwa der Faust – und erlernten Zeichen – wie etwa dem Victory-V Winston Churchills – zuweilen fliessend, wie etwa bei der Stopp-Geste des Verkehrspolizisten. Diesen Handdarstellungen auf dem Plakat ist jedoch gemeinsam, dass die Hand eine Form annimmt, die wir deuten müssen, und es ist weniger die spezifische Hand als die Form, die sie bildet, die als kommunikatives Zeichen das Plakat bestimmt. Auffallend ist, dass es bei diesen Darstellungen – ganz anders als bei den Handmodels – eigentlich nicht um individuelle Hände geht. Die Hand, die hier auftritt, trägt keinen Damenhandschuh, keinen Ehering; sie entspricht dem zumeist patriarchalischen, eurozentrischen Mainstream der weissen Männerhand im besten Mannesalter, quasi als «Normalfall»

B Das Handmodel Emily Grimson

C Handformen in der Höhle von El Castillo.
Foto: Pedro Saura

der Abbildung einer Hand. Sie kann sogar, wenn die Geste bekannt genug ist oder durch eine schriftliche Verdoppelung noch einmal benannt wird, als Umriss verdoppelt werden und ist nun aller Individualität beraubt 77.

THE FAMILY OF MAN

Noch anonymer wird die Hand, wenn schliesslich nur noch ihr Abdruck zu sehen ist oder ihr Umriss. Schon mit der zweiten Gruppe von Handdarstellungen – den handelnden Händen – wurde ja bereits etwas sichtbar von der Hand als Universalwerkzeug des Menschen. Nur weniges, was wir Menschen tun, wird nicht auch mit den Händen getan. Kaum etwas ist typischer für den Menschen als die Hand und ihr universaler Gebrauch, kaum etwas unterscheidet ihn prägnanter körperlich von anderen Tieren, kaum etwas deutet damit auch so universell auf den Menschen als Teil der Menschheit hin. Alle Menschen haben Hände, alle Menschen gebrauchen Hände, und damit kann die Hand auch für eine universelle Teilhabe an der Menschheit stehen.

Diese Überlegung führt schliesslich zur vierten Gruppe von Händen auf dem Plakat, und dieser Bildtopos hat eine noch längere Geschichte als die der Hand des antiken Verkäufers – wenn nicht sogar die längste denkbare Bildgeschichte überhaupt. Denn als die frühen Menschen begannen, Bilder auf Höhlenwände zu bannen, waren es die Umrisse ihrer Hände, die sie als Schablonen einsetzten. In der Cueva de El Castillo (40.000 v. Chr.), dem derzeit ältesten bekannten Fundort menschengemachter Bilder, kann man sie bewundern C. Aber sie flankieren auch die anatomisch präzisen Tierdarstellungen in der Grotte Chauvet (30.000–22.000 v. Chr.) oder dienen unabhängig von diesen viele tausend Jahre später als Muster in der Cueva de las Manos in Argentinien (7000–1000 v. Chr.). Mit Ocker, Holzkohle und Rötel hielten hier die Menschen die Form ihrer Hände fest wie frühe Fotogramme. Damit bannten sie die Umrisse jenes Körperteils auf die Wand, mit dem sie zeichneten und jagten, und damit eben jenen, der sie vom Tier unterscheidet. Diese Universalgeste der Hand, diese Feststellung «Ich bin ein Mensch», wird noch heute verstanden und schafft auch heute noch eine seltsame Verbindung zu den Bildern früher Menschen.

Von der anthropologischen Feststellung «Ich bin ein Mensch» zur humanistischen Erkenntnis «Wir sind allesamt Menschen» ist es dann nur noch ein kurzer Weg. In dieser Funktion als Signet der Menschheit selbst taucht die Hand als Bildtopos insbesondere in der zweiten Hälfte des 20. Jahrhunderts wieder auf. Die Hand formt nun nicht mehr ein Zeichen, die Hand wird selbst zum Zeichen. Die gespreizte Hand steht jetzt für ein idealistisches «Wir alle», für das Universelle des Menschen, letztlich also die schwärmerische Idee einer globalen Menschheit – und bildet hierbei auch erwartbare Untergruppen aus wie etwa den Umriss der Kinderhand, der für Kinder an sich steht, und die bunte Ausführung der Hand, die für die Vielfalt des Menschengeschlechts stehen soll.

HAND AUFS HERZ!

Hinter der motivischen Gemeinsamkeit der Hand verbergen sich – wie wir gesehen haben – also ganz unterschiedliche Funktionsweisen: Die Hand des Handmodels kann indexikalisch auf die Seife verweisen oder als rhetorische Figur der Metonymie am Radioknopf drehen, Hände können als Symbol zur Revolution aufrufen oder als Ikon für die Friedensbewegung werben.

Doch gibt es – neben der motivischen Gemeinsamkeit – noch eine gestalterisch-funktionale Besonderheit der Hand auf dem Plakat, die allen diesen Gruppen gemeinsam ist: Die Hand ist ein «schnelles Bild», weil jeder sie kennt. Eine Hand ist eine Hand ist eine Hand. Die Hand muss – ähnlich wie Auge, Mund, Sonne, Mond, Baum, Herz und so weiter – nicht erst zeitraubend erkannt und dechiffriert werden. Sie ist ein leicht verfügbares Zeichen im Repertoire der Gestaltung, ein solides zudem, das robust und unmittelbar kommunizieren kann und damit einer wesentlichen Eigenschaft des Plakats sehr entgegenkommt. Denn in der grossen Familie der grafischen Erzeugnisse gehört das Plakat, wenn es nicht gerade ein Leseplakat ist, zum Familienzweig der Kommunikatoren mit hohem Tempo. Aufmerksamkeit erzeugen, Inhalte kompakt kommunizieren, rasch erfassbar sein ist seine Aufgabe, und es ist die hohe Kunst, hierbei «schnelle Bilder» zu verwenden, ohne ins Klischee zu kippen. Die Beispiele dieser Sammlung lassen sich demnach auch in dieser Richtung lesen: als typische Plakate, die schnell, robust und effektvoll eine Botschaft übermitteln wollen. Und hierfür ein spezielles Sujet nutzen, das dazu in besonderer Weise in der Lage ist: die Hand.

1 Dene Barnett u. a., «Gestik», in: *Historisches Wörterbuch der Rhetorik*, Bd. 3, Darmstadt 1996, Sp. 972–989.

8 **Percy Wenger (zugeschrieben)**
Vin Vaudois/Vin doré
1946

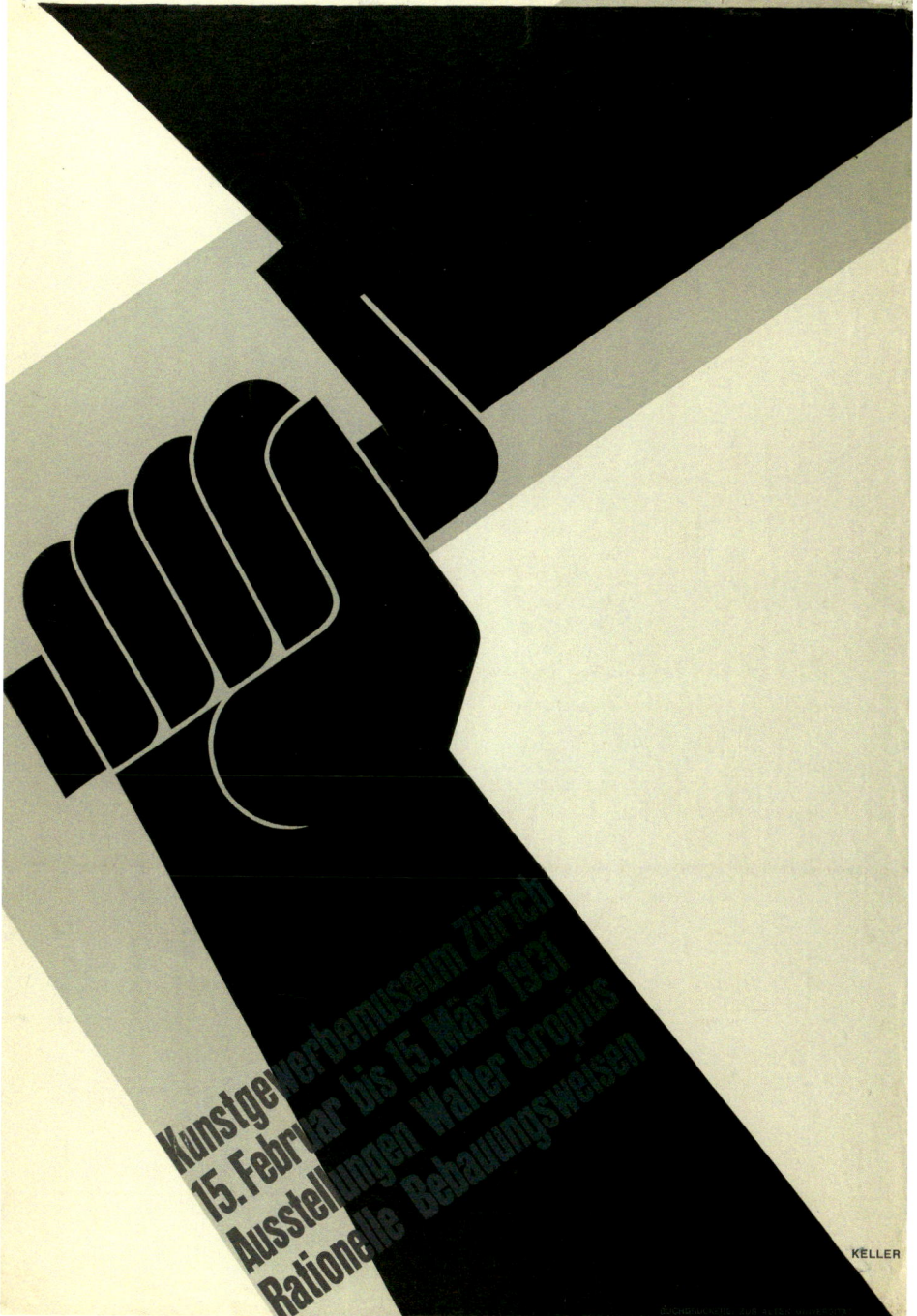

9 **Ernst Keller**
Kunstgewerbemuseum Zürich/
Ausstellungen Walter Gropius/Rationelle
Bebauungsweisen
1931

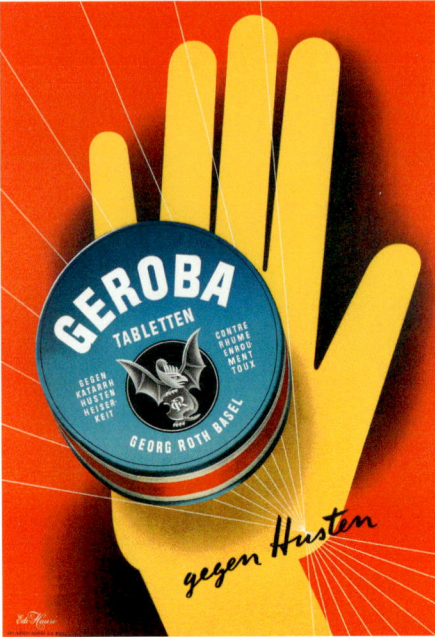

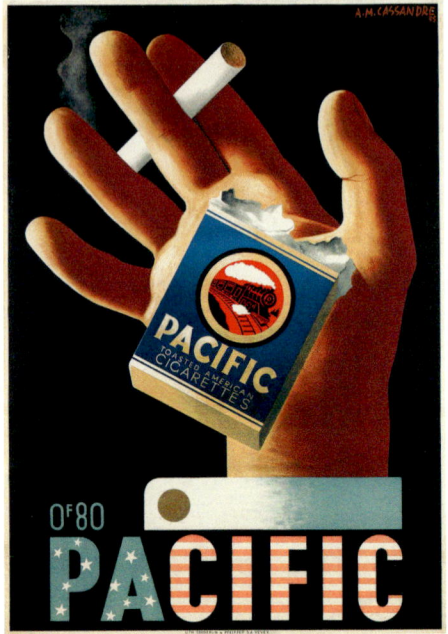

10 **Edi Hauri**
Geroba Tabletten / Gegen Husten
1936

11 **Hannes Portmann**
Photo: Willi S. Eberle
Vivi-Kola / Mit Eglisauer Mineralwasser, 1957

12 **Adolphe Mouron Cassandre**
Pacific
1935

13 **Hermann Eidenbenz**
Süssmost ist gesund
1951

14 **Charles Kuhn**
Téléphone international
1930

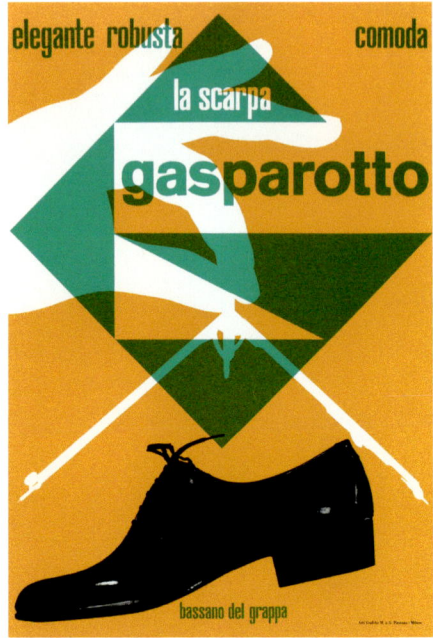

15 **Hans Neuburg**
Das Zeichen für handwerkliche Massarbeit
1950

16 **anonym**
Olivetti Lexikon Elettrica
1961

17 **Heinz Waibl**
La scarpa Gasparotto/Elegante/Robusta/Comoda
1959

18 **Walter Bangerter/Klaus Fischer**
Bigla Stahlmöbel/Büro-Organisationen/Oberholzer
Zürich, 1954

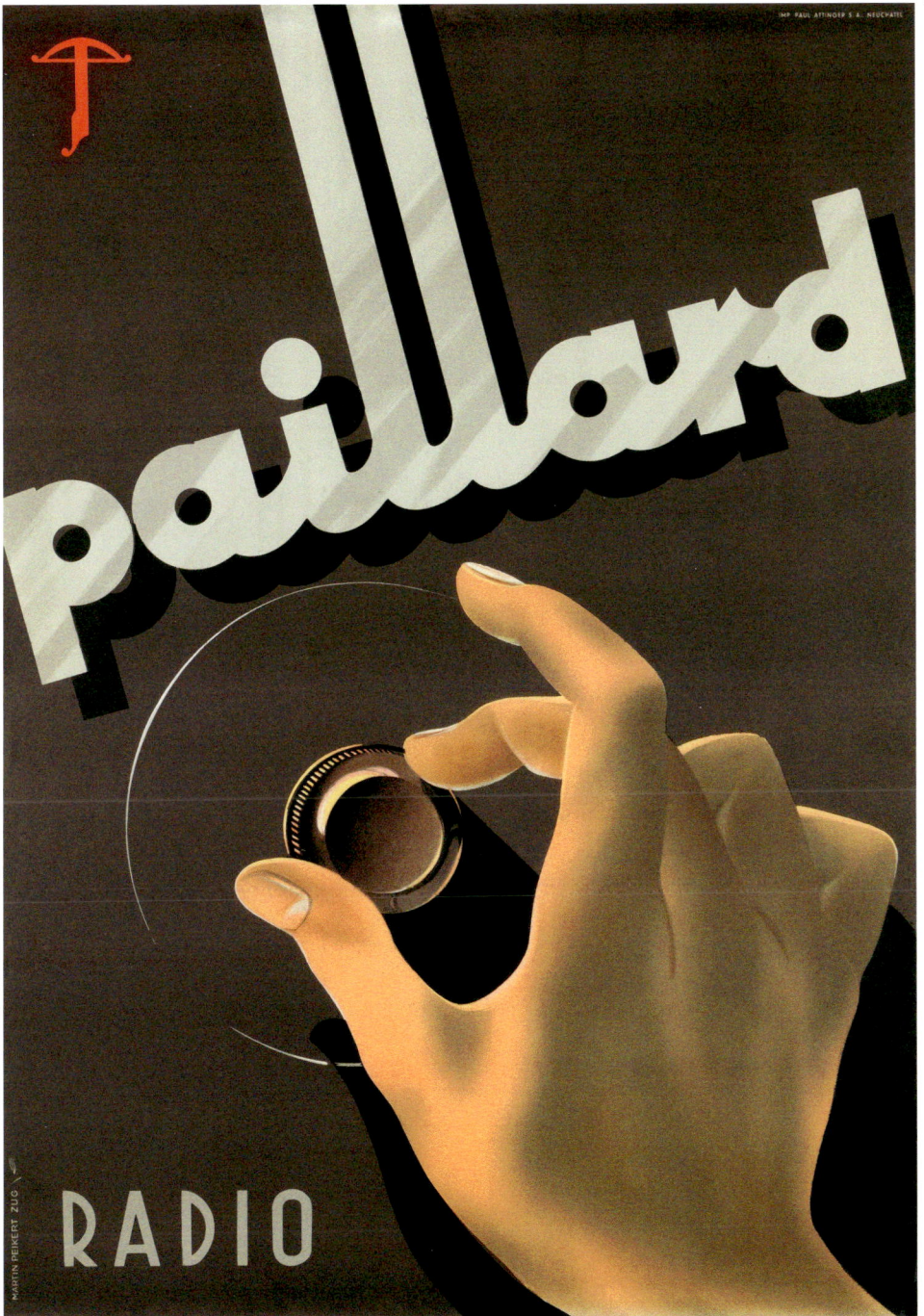

19 **Martin Peikert**
Paillard Radio
1937

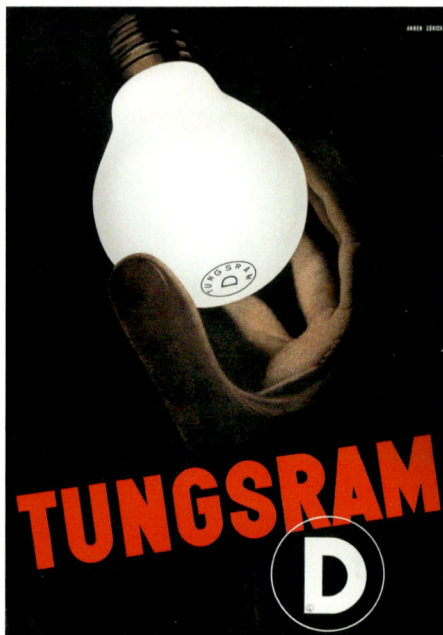

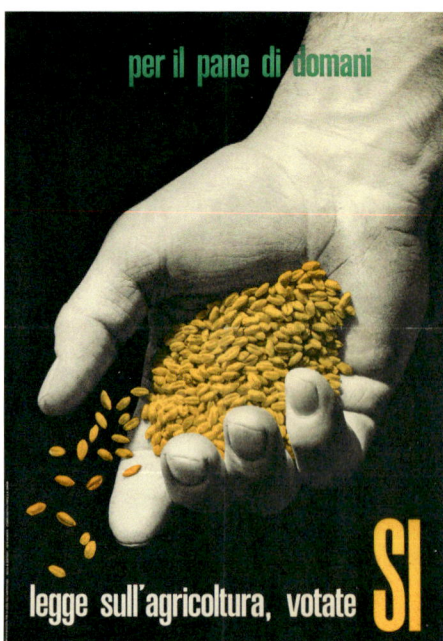

20 **Heinrich Steiner**
Photo: Ernst Albrecht Heiniger
Téléphonez, 1939

21 **Arno Löffler**
Trinkt mehr Milch!
1937

22 **Melchior Annen**
Tungsram D, 1937

23 **Willi Günthart-Maag**
Photo: Ernst Albrecht Heiniger
Per il pane di domani / Legge sull' agricoltura, votate sí
1952

24 **Viktor Rutz**
Floralp Butter am besten
1939

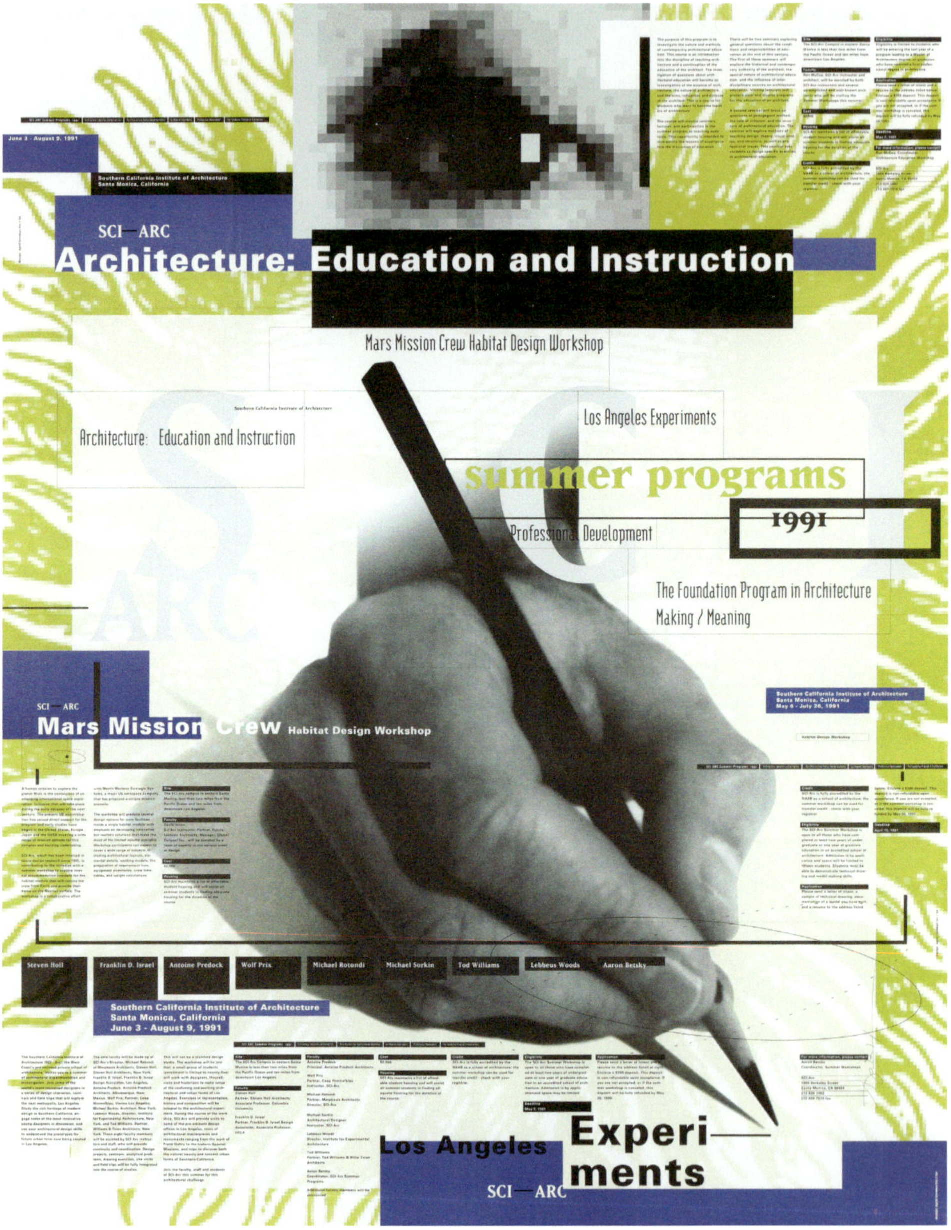

25 **April Greiman**
Summer Programs 1991
1991

26 **Frédéric Henri Kay Henrion**
Design at Home
1949

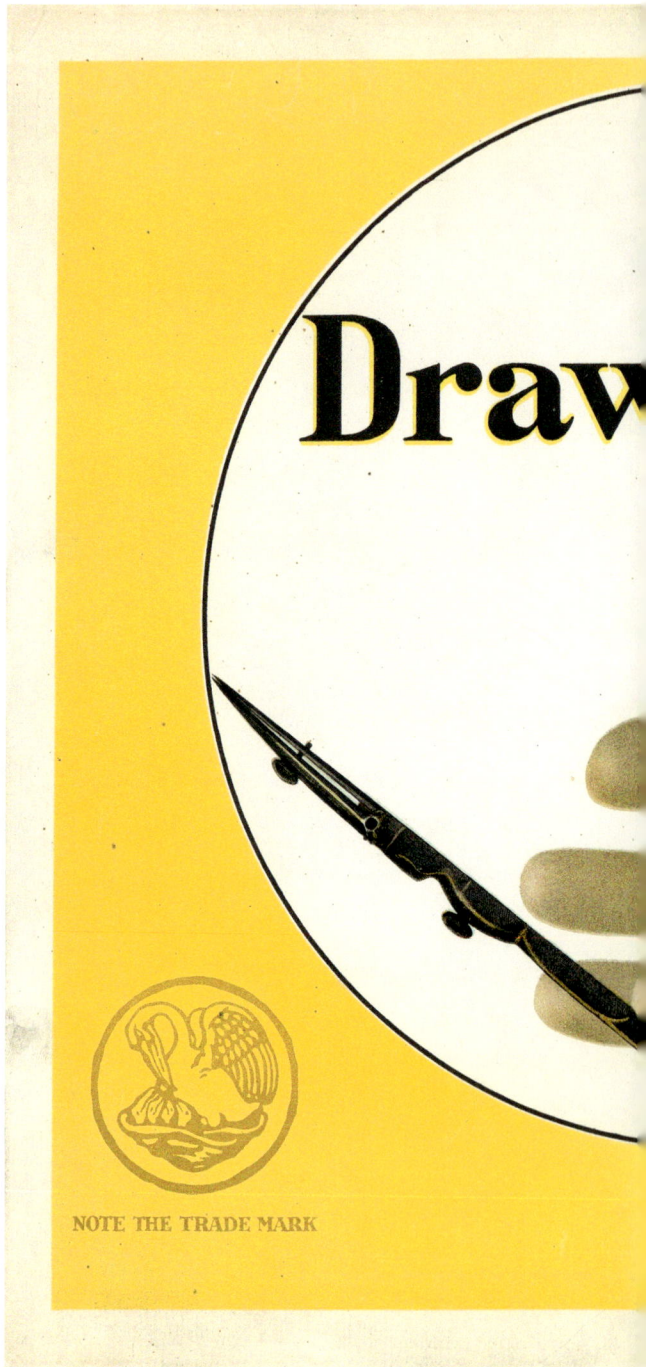

NOTE THE TRADE MARK

27 **El' Lisickij**
Pelican Drawing Ink.
1925

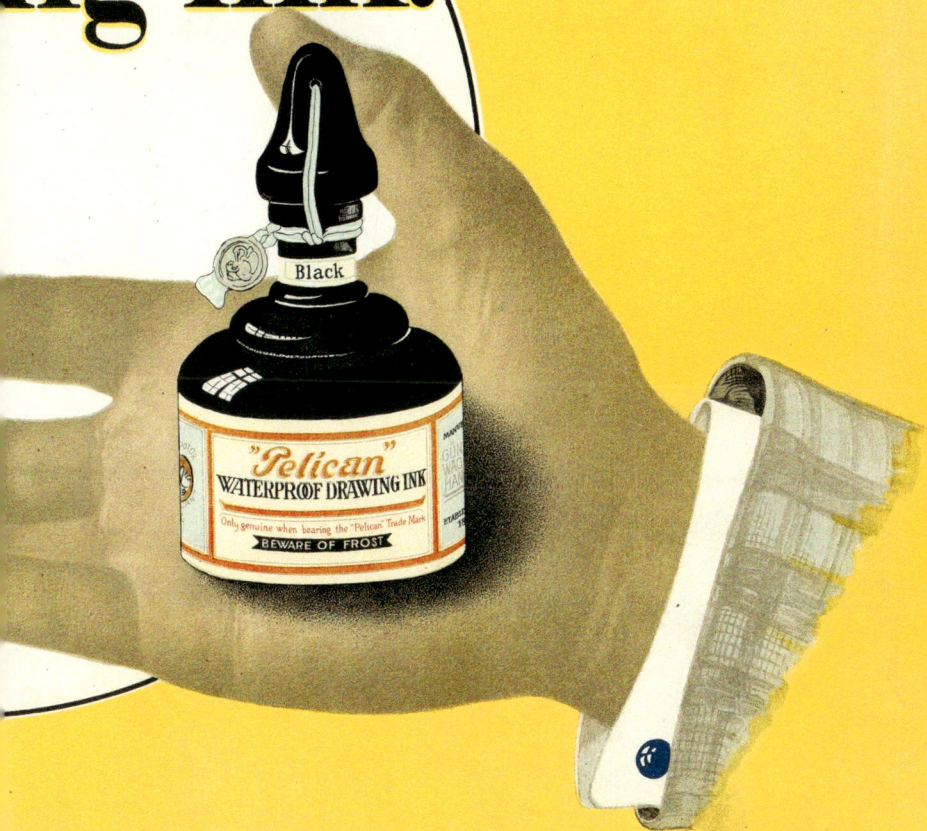

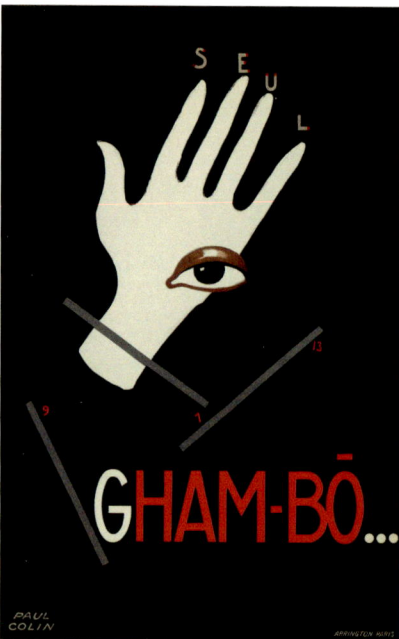

28, 29, 30 **Otl Aicher**

Wann endlich Europa?, 1951

Ein Jahrhundert bittet um Frieden, 1948

Weltwirtschaft, 1948

31 **Paul Colin**
Gham-bō …/Seul
1930

32 **Otl Aicher**
Der europäische Familienzwist
1951

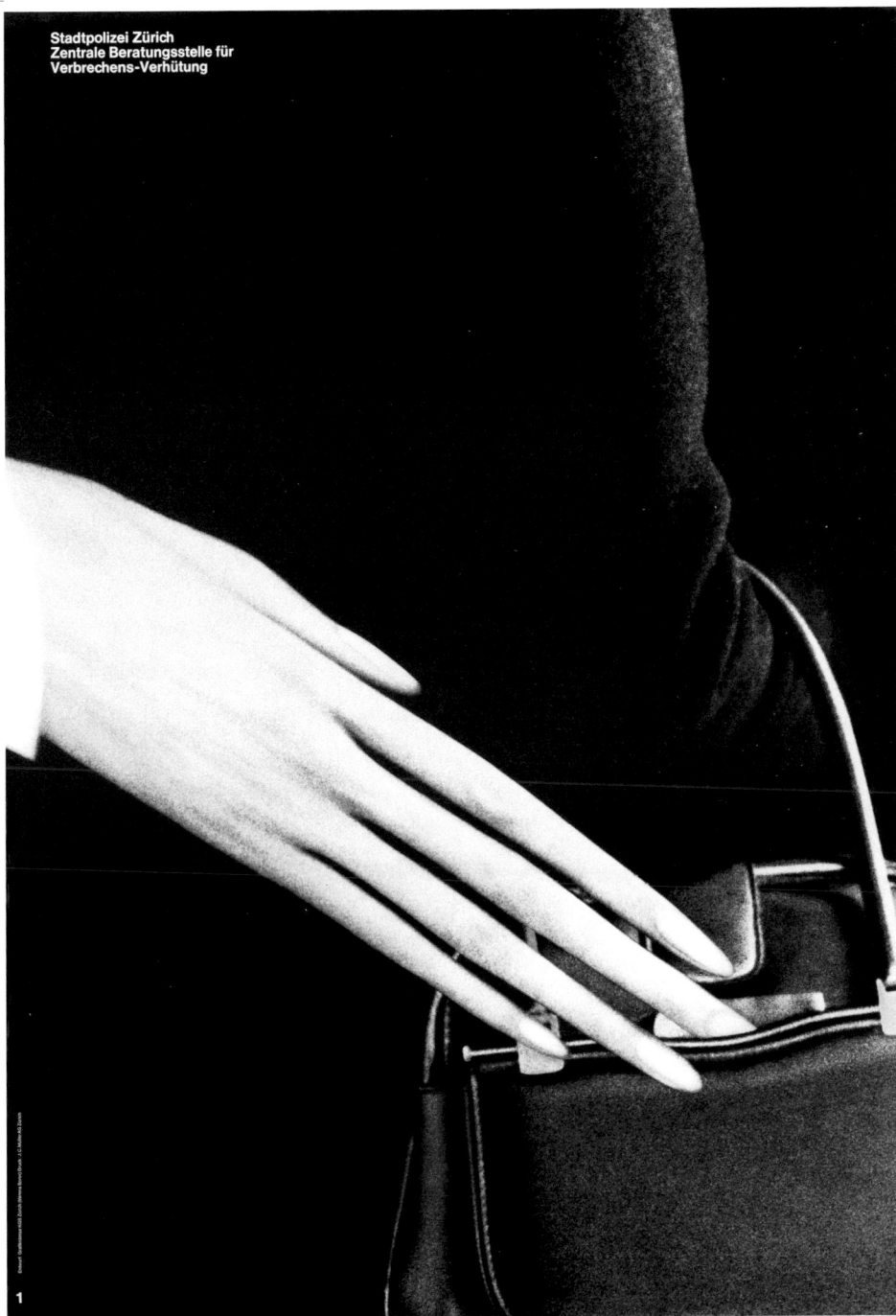

Stadtpolizei Zürich
Zentrale Beratungsstelle für
Verbrechens-Verhütung

33 **anonym**
Stadtpolizei Zürich/Zentrale Beratungsstelle
für Verbrechens-Verhütung
1967

34 **Viktor Rutz**
Wer rechnet, kauft im Globus
1937

35 **Robert Siebold**
Vorsicht
ca. 1987

36 **anonym**
Razoblacim i uničtožim provokatorov i rasprostranitelej
paničeskich sluchov
1941

37 **Atelier Populaire**
Le vote ne change rien / La lutte continue
1968

38 **Roy Lichtenstein**
Amerikansk Pop-konst / Moderna Museet
1965

39 **Shigeo Fukuda**
Shigeo Fukuda / The Ginza Tokyo
1979

40 **Karl Gerstner**
Auch Du bist liberal
1956

41 **Shigeo Fukuda**
Shigeo Fukuda / Illustrick
1990

Für
Ihre
Sicherheit
nur
dieses
Überkleid

42 **Bernhard Lüthi**
Für Ihre Sicherheit nur dieses Überkleid
ca. 1966

43 **Digby Wills Ltd.**
The new ‹Zebra› crossings / Respect them / Use them
1950

44 **Hans Hartmann**
Handzeichen schaffen Klarheit
1936

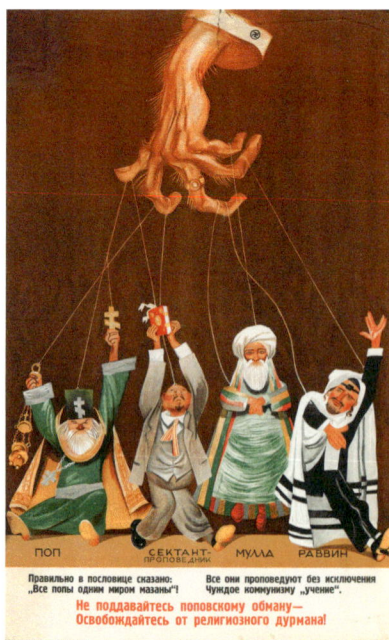

45 **C. E. Gogler**
Confiscation de la propriété/Non
1922

46 **Lucian Bernhard**
Tretet ein in den Grenzschutz Ost!
Schützt die Heimat gegen Bolschewismus!, 1919

47 **Fritz Rosen**
Starke Hand – rettet das Land
ca. 1932

48 **Michail Michajlovič Čeremnych**
Pravil'no v poslovice skazano:
«Vse popy odnim mirom mazany»!, 1938

49 **Atelier Populaire**
Université Populaire Été 68
1968

50 **Peter von Arx / Peter Olpe**
Kunst und Politik
1971

51 **anonym**
Heraus zum 1. Mai / POCH
1975

52 **Gregor Huber / Ivan Sterzinger**
Talk to the Hand
2013

53 **Eric Andersen**
1. Mai 2014 / Mit einer geballten Faust
kann man keinen Händedruck wechseln. 2014

54 **Eric Andersen**
1. Mai 2014 / Mit einer geballten Faust
kann man keinen Händedruck wechseln.
2014

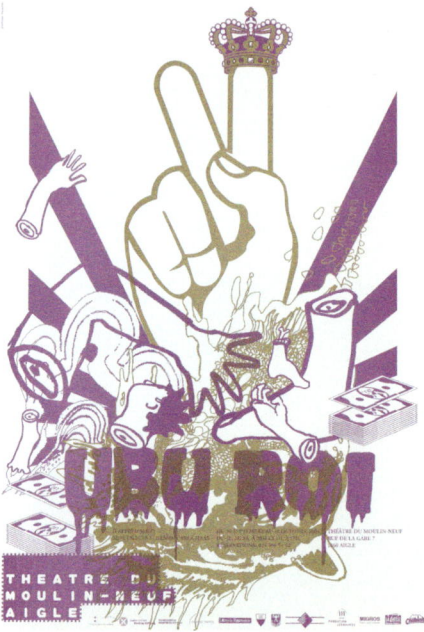

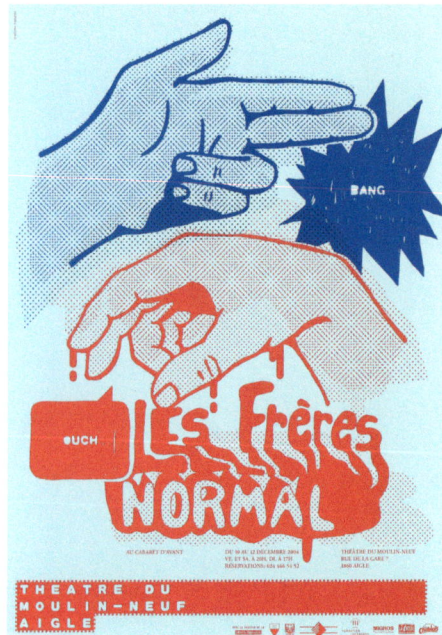

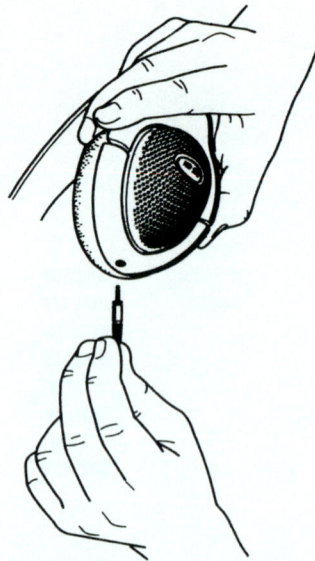

55 **Cédric Henny/Patrick Monnier/Violène Pont**
Ubu Roi
2004

56 **Cédric Henny/Patrick Monnier/Violène Pont**
Les frères normal
2004

57 **Ruedi Wyss**
Eine japanische Nacht/Jazz Now Bern
1984

58 **Lukas Zimmermann**
[ohne Text]
2002

59 **Bastien Aubry/Dimitri Broquard**
Theater hat Nebenwirkungen
2004

THE ACTIVE POSTER:
ON THE VISUAL RHETORIC OF THE HAND ON ADVERTISING POSTERS

Arne Scheuermann

HAND MODELS AND MODEL HANDS

In the comedy *You Don't Mess with the Zohan* (USA, 2008, directed by Dennis Dugan), the celebrated Israeli superagent Zohan Dvir flees in frustration from the war and conflict in his homeland in order to realize his dream career in New York: becoming a hairdresser. But things aren't easy at first. Disappointed by his initial setbacks, he decides to get started by working as a salesman in an electronics store called "Going Out of Business." But its owner tries to talk him out of it. "The electronics store is a dream killer," says the boss, looking out over his employees, and he explains what they all had really wanted to do before their unfulfilled American dreams forced them into the daily grind of selling electronics. One wanted to be a race car driver, another a comedian. "Yosi wanted to be a hand model," he continues bleakly, and we see a mature man with a beard and a high forehead showing a customer a mobile phone with supple, deliberate gestures. He holds the phone relaxed in one hand while pointing out its merits with the other, his elegance reminiscent of the TV sales channels where presenters show off watches, knife sets and vacuum cleaners A. The intended meaning is clear: if this shop is able to destroy the dreams of such a gifted hand model, just think what could befall the hero with his dreams of becoming a hairdresser.

"Hand model" as a profession actually exists. And as we learn from the above scene, despite its exaggerated parody, success in this profession is the result of various factors. A beautiful hand alone is not enough, nor is perseverance, talent or a lucky breakthrough. People with beautiful hands also need to be able to demonstrate and make a "pitch" B. They need to have mastered gestures in order to be able to carry out these tasks elegantly. They need to be able to perform all the oscillatory movements and pointing gestures that direct the gaze of the observer and show goods in a proper light. Above all, this means that the hand alone sells nothing. It needs something that it can present: merchandise.

The profession of a hand model thus probably has its origins in the marketplace thousands of years ago. "Look here–have you ever held such fine material in your hands? Come here! See for yourself! Check it out yourself!" The seller strokes the material with his hand, gently holding the seam, pointing to the pattern of the weave, testing its sturdiness by rubbing the material between his thumb and middle finger. And alongside the glib salesmen with the gift of gab, it is quite conceivable that those who could use the rhetoric of elegant gestures to get their merchandise noticed also enjoyed an advantage in the ancient marketplace.

The hand that "talks up" the goods might thus be as old as trade itself. And so it should not surprise us that when advertising posters first emerged, they showed hands holding the goods, "pitching" them, using the products and offering them for sale. In the heyday of advertising photography, the trend was increasingly to have professional hand models present watches, hold packs of cigarettes and point to washing powders. And the physiognomy of the model's hands had to be ideologically appropriate to the goods in question: the hand holding the cognac glass had to be robustly masculine, the back of it covered in manly hair, while soap had to be held between the thumb and index finger of a slender woman's hand.

THE GLOVE THAT FITS THE HAND

This principle of appropriateness—called *aptum*—is also central to the discipline of rhetoric. The type of language used and the object in question must always be closely in tune if a speech is going to convince. The content must be appropriate to the level of affect of its presentation if the speech is to awaken feelings successfully. Since antiquity, these systems of rules have encompassed not just the composition of speeches, the theory of rhetorical figures and the techniques of learning speeches by heart, but also the efficacious, emotional manner in which the speech is given. It should not surprise us that rhetoric has developed a highly elaborate system of gestures over the course of the centuries. After all, it is not just about testing goods in the marketplace. In courts of law and in parliaments, too, speakers gesture to their allies and point an accusatory index finger at their opponents. Over time—and especially since the early modern period—this rhetoric of speakers' gestures has been further developed and adapted for use in the theater, in operas and in sermons.

The concepts of *natura*, *ars* and *exercitio*—the naturalness of gestures, their skillful employment and repeated practice as the basis of their mastery—allowed for the development of comprehensive, highly specialized books of rules for priests, opera singers and dramatic actors. These regulated in great detail what topics in a speech should prompt one to open one's hand and point to the heavens; when one should strike one's breast with a closed fist; and when the open palms should be used to accompany a shrug of the shoulders. We still come across these gestures today when we look at old drawings and paintings. We understand some of them spontaneously as if they were from our own time. In the case of others, we often need a competent "translation" in order to understand their meaning. Several of these hands in art history have been brought together on the poster "Ich bin Rahmen für Handlung" ("I Frame Action"), where they are all humorously turned into pointing gestures 6.

The gestures of actors, preachers and singers awaken emotions in those speakers (or singers) who use them. There is a physiological connection that we can comprehend by testing the gestures ourselves. Try making a declaration of love with clenched fists or insulting someone with your hands relaxed and pointing upwards! Similarly, these

A

gestures also prompt emotions in the observer and the listener, structure a lecture, provide emphasis in the course of a speech and enable the audience to identify with what is expressed.

There is a large repertoire of such gestures. In the *Historisches Wörterbuch der Rhetorik*, for example—which is our basic source for an overview of rhetoric research—at least five basic types of gestures are summed up and differentiated: indicative, imitative and expressive gestures, gestures of emphasis and gestures of address.[1] The gestures of the hand model, for example, would be assigned to the first of these categories. The beauty of the hand and the effectiveness of its pointing gestures are paramount, and the symbols used here are primarily indexical. This should not surprise us either, since "index" in Latin means the index finger. But as we shall demonstrate later, even hands on posters that are not actually touting merchandise can be understood as gestures and can be assigned, for example, to the categories of expressive and emphatic gestures.

Nevertheless—and here we come back to our examples—not all hands on posters can be reduced to the concept of gesture. Many such hands do not gesticulate at all: they act, make signs or simply represent humanity in general, thanks to their immediately recognizable, universal form.

ACTING HANDS

This brings us to the second group of hand motifs. Besides the hands that present and "advertise"—in other words, those hands that in fact duplicate the function of the poster (itself a medium of pointing) by actually using pointing gestures—there are hands on the posters in this collection whose function is less to tout merchandise than to use objects. While the hand that holds a cigarette depicts what we might consider a borderline case here, other hands put crosses on ballot papers, steal wallets, grasp hammers and pick up telephones. Hands hold chopsticks and pens, adjust the knobs on a radio and sow seeds. Here the hands fulfill different functions: sometimes they grip something as an extension of the arm, at other times they are the base of the fingers with their fine motor skills.

A Film still from *You Don't Mess with the Zohan*
(USA, 2008)

48

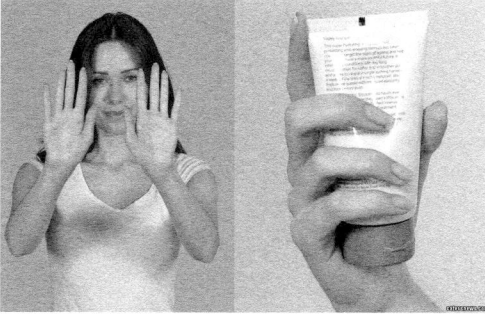
B

C

And yet in these depictions it is not unusual for the hand to be less significant than its actions. What is really conveyed is not the hand using a dial, but the act of making a telephone call. As a visual rhetorical figure of metonymy, in such cases the hand stands for the action in which it is involved: the focus is on casting a vote, pickpocketing, handicrafts, eating, writing, listening to the radio and sowing seeds.

The active hand thus becomes a potential metaphor for work in general. Working people—those members of the population who use their hands on their jobs—are represented by the raised scythe, the swinging hammer. The action becomes a gesture, and the gesture becomes a symbol.

STOP! GO! VIVE LA RÉVOLUTION!
This brings us to a third group of hand topoi. These hand depictions could be described in general as speaking gestures. They are directed at observers as if the poster were their living counterpart. The raised hand whose gesture commands us to stop, the hand that greedily tries to seize our savings, the fist that calls us to revolution (because, if needed, it can strike a blow): in all these examples the hand forms a symbol that should be understood as such. Here the transitions between expressive gestures (such as the fist) and symbols we have learned (such as Winston Churchill's "V for victory") can be fluid, as with the "stop" gesture of the traffic policeman. What all these hand depictions on posters have in common is that the hand takes on a form that we have to interpret. It is not so much the hand itself, but its form that, as a communicative symbol, determines the meaning of the poster. It is also noteworthy that in these depictions—which are very different from those of our hand models—it is not the individual hand that is significant. Here the hand does not wear a woman's glove or a wedding ring, but corresponds to the mostly patriarchal, Eurocentric mainstream, namely, the hand of a mature white male. In other words, it represents a "typical" depiction of a hand. If its gesture is sufficiently well known or if it is described tautologically in words, it can even be given in outlines and is then deprived of all individuality 77.

B The hand model Emily Grimson

C Hand shapes in the cave of El Castillo.
Photo: Pedro Saura

THE FAMILY OF MAN

The hand becomes even more anonymous if only a handprint or the outline of a hand can be seen. The second group of hand depictions—the acting hands—already hinted at the hand's significance as a universal tool of mankind. There is little that humans do that is not done with their hands. There is hardly anything more typical of humans than their hands and their universal use; there is hardly anything that separates us more clearly from other animals in terms of our physical being; there is hardly anything else that so universally signifies a man or woman as a member of humankind. All human beings have hands, all people use their hands and thus the hand can stand for the universal sharing of what it is to be human.

This consideration ultimately leads us to the fourth group of hands on posters, and this visual topos has an even longer history than that of the hand of the market seller in ancient times. It might even have the longest conceivable pictorial history of all. After all, when early humans began to draw images on the walls of caves, they did so by using the outlines of their hands as templates. We can admire these today in the Cueva de El Castillo (40,000 BC), which is currently the oldest-known site of human--made images C. In the Chauvet Cave (30,000–22,000 BC), such images are flanked by anatomically precise depictions of animals. Thousands of years later, hands served as templates in the Cueva de las Manos in Argentina (the "Cave of Hands," 7,000–1,000 BC). There, using ochre, charcoal and red chalk, people preserved the form of their hands as if in early photograms. On the walls they captured the contours of that part of their anatomy that they used to draw and hunt; in other words, the part of their body that distinguished them from animals. This universal gesture of the hand, this declaration that "I am a human being," is still understood in this manner today and creates an extraordinary connection between us and the images of these early people.

It is only a short step from the anthropological observation that "I am a human being" to the humanist realization that "we are all human beings." In its function as a mark of humanity itself, the hand emerges again as a visual topos above all in the second half of the twentieth century. The hand no longer merely forms a symbol: the hand itself becomes a symbol. The outspread hand stands for an idealistic "we," for "all of us," for the universalism of humanity and thus ultimately for the enthusiastic concept of a global humanity. At the same time, it also forms the subgroups we might expect, such as the outline of a child's hand standing for "children" and a hand rendered in bright colors representing the diversity of the whole human race.

HAND ON HEART!

As we have seen, behind the common hand motifs lie very different functions: the hand of the hand model can point indexically to a bar of soap or turn the knob on a radio as a rhetorical figure of metonymy; hands can call us to revolution or serve as an icon of the peace movement.

And yet, besides these commonalities, the hand used on posters has a special, functional design feature that is shared by all these groups. The hand is a "quick image" because everyone knows it. A hand is a hand is a hand. It takes no time for the hand—like the eye, mouth, sun, moon, tree, heart, etc.—to be recognized and decoded. It is a symbol that is readily available in the design repertoire, a very solid symbol that can communicate robustly and immediately and thus conforms to one of the fundamental characteristics of a poster. After all, within the large family of graphic products, the poster—if it is not a textual poster intended to be read—ensures quick communication. Its task is to generate attention, to communicate content in a compact form and to be easily comprehensible. The art of the poster is the art of using such "quick images" without falling into clichés. The examples in this collection can thus also be read as typical posters that aim to convey a message quickly, robustly and effectively. And for this they use a special subject that is especially suitable for this purpose: the hand.

1 Dene Barnett et al., "Gestik," in *Historisches Wörterbuch der Rhetorik,* vol. 3, Darmstadt 1996, cols. 972–989; also Dene Barnett, *The Art of Gesture,* Heidelberg 1987, 27–8.

60 **Richard Paul Lohse**
Photo: Ernst Albrecht Heiniger
Deine Zeitung – das Volksrecht
1942

61 **Klaus Wittkugel**
Arbeiter! In die Partei der Arbeiter!
1956

62 **Gustav Gustavovič Klucis**
Vypolnim plan velikich rabot
1930

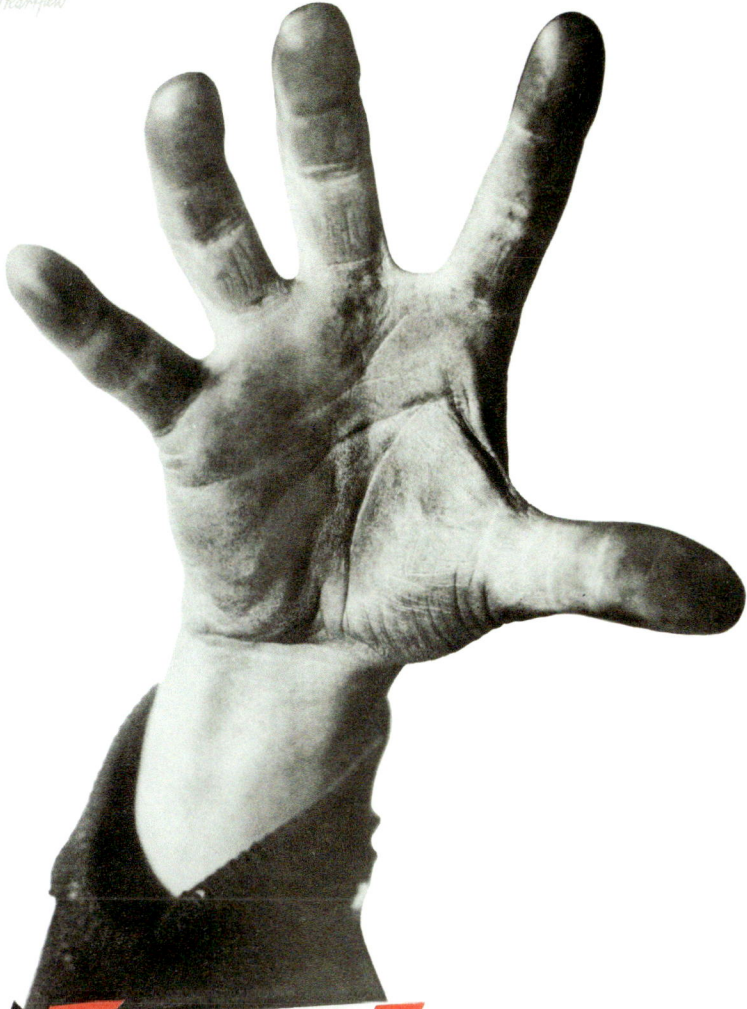

5 Finger hat die Hand
Mit **5** packst Du den Feind!
Wählt Liste **5** Kommunistische Partei!

63 **John Heartfield**
5 Finger hat die Hand
1928, Nachdruck 1976

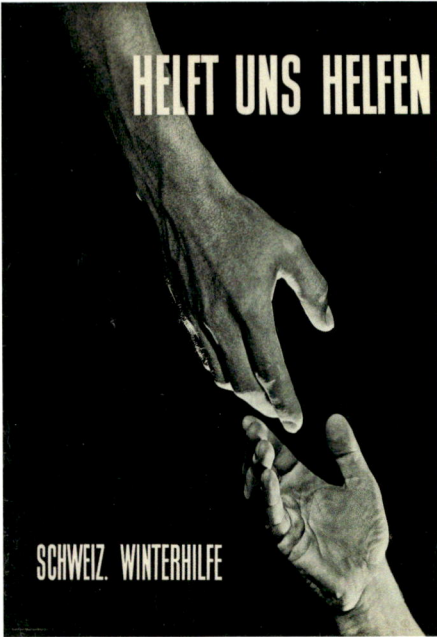

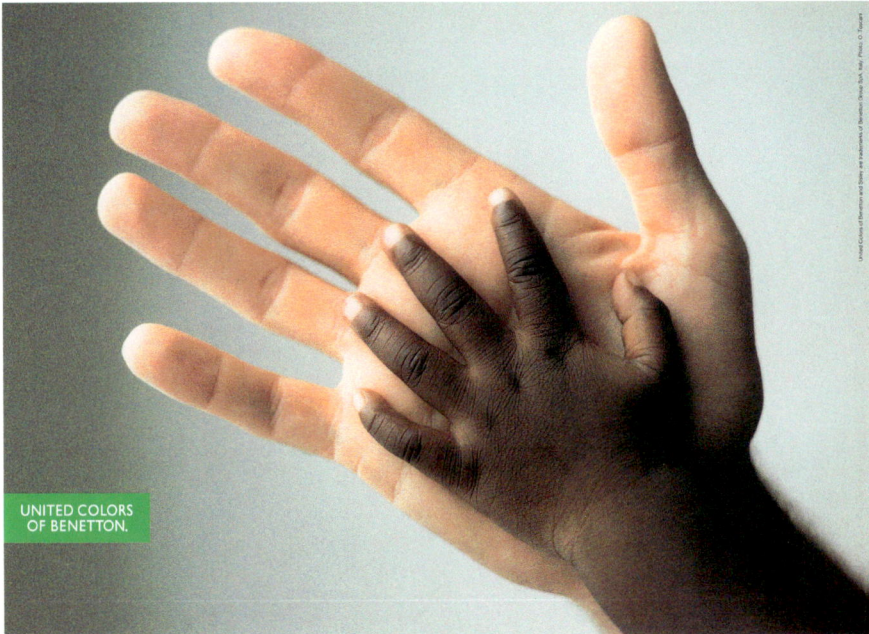

64 **Richard Paul Lohse**
Helft uns helfen, 1940

65 **Oliviero Toscani**
United Colors of Benetton
1990

66 **René Schmid**
Photo: Karl Keller
Eine Versicherungspolice ist .../... eine Sicherheit, 1966

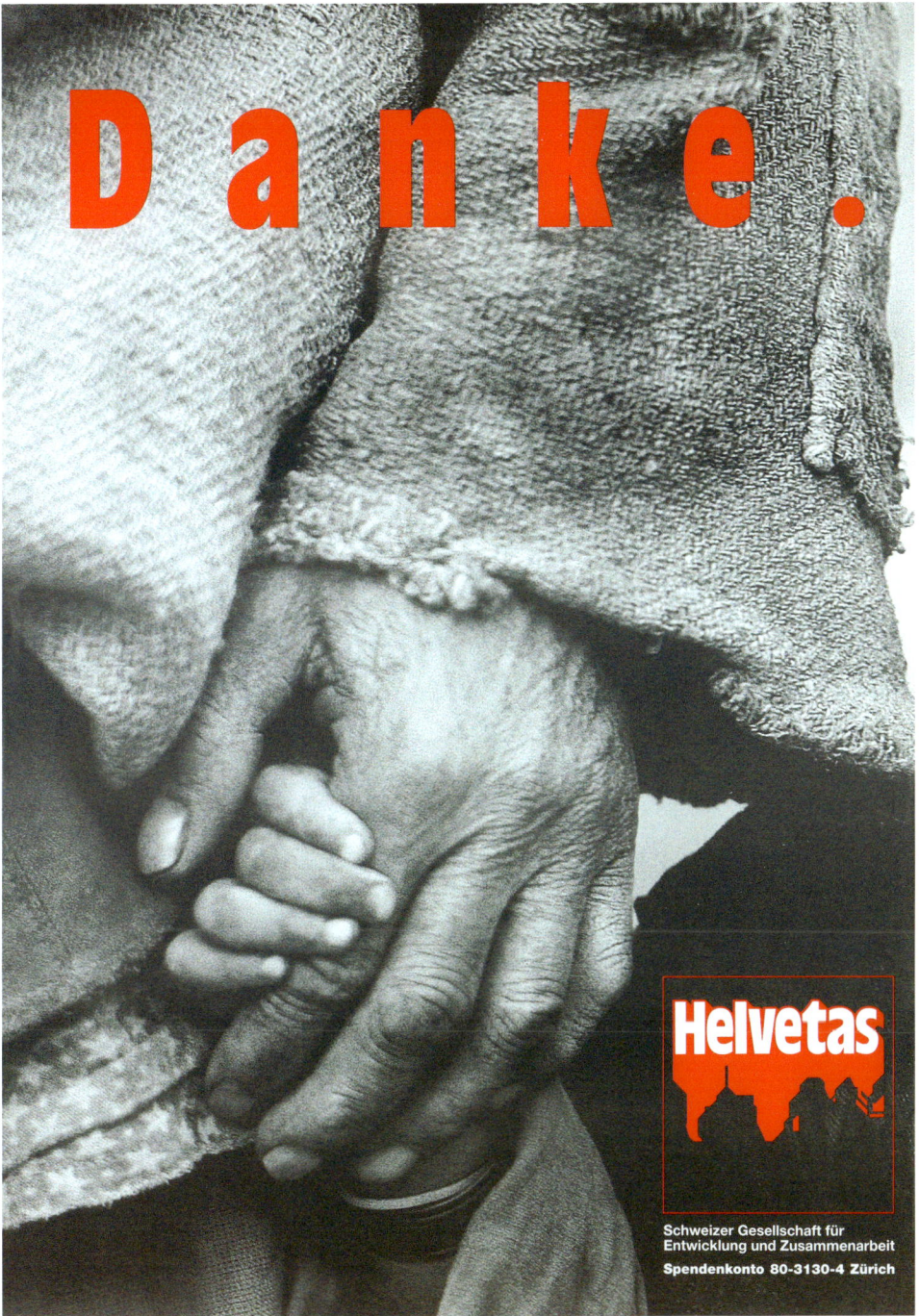

67 **Heidi Franceschini**
Danke. Helvetas
ca. 1991

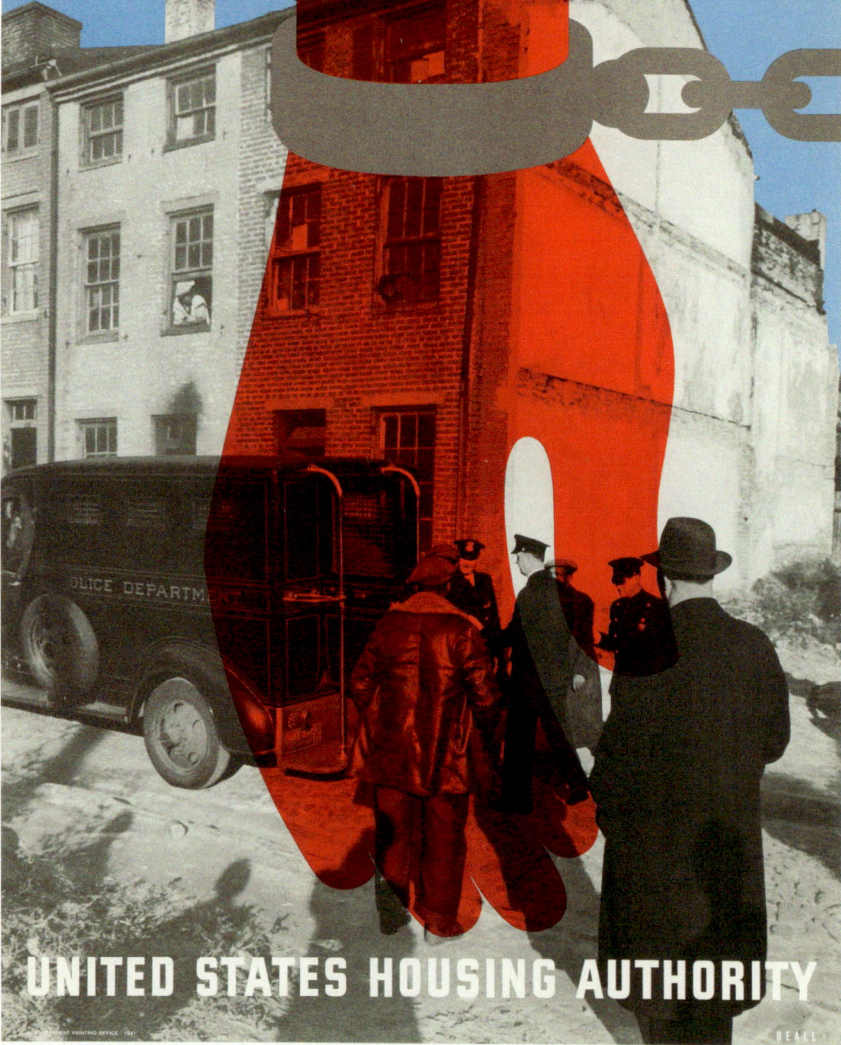

68 **Lester Beall**
Slums Breed Crime
1941

69 **Lester Beall**
Cross out Slums
1941

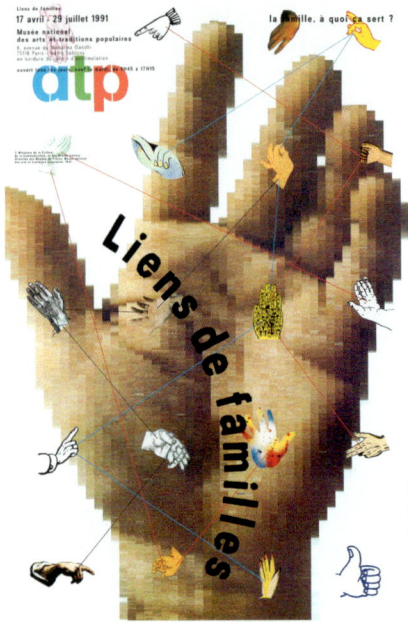

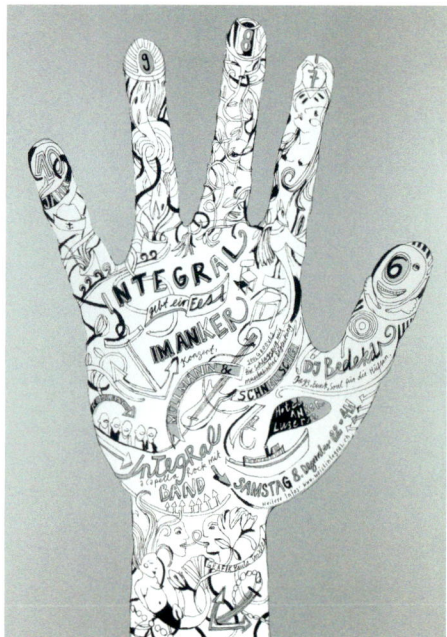

70 Les Graphistes Associés
Liens de familles/La famille, à quoi ça sert?
1991

71 Ueli Kleeb/Caroline Lötscher
7 Tage Auferstehen in den 17 Zuger Pfarreien
2006

72 Ueli Kleeb/Caroline Lötscher
Pfarrei St. Jakobus der Ältere Cham
2006

73 Paula Troxler
Integral gibt ein Fest im Anker
2007

Erratum

Regrettably, the photograph "Vanunu M was hijacked in Rome ITL" was incorrectly attributed to the designer David Tartakover, who merely used it as a template for one of his posters. This results in the corrections below. This error will be revised in the next edition of the book.

Bedauerlicherweise wurde die Fotografie «Vanunu M was hijacked in Rome ITL» dem Gestalter David Tartakover zugeschrieben, der diese lediglich als Vorlage für eines seiner Plakate verwendet hat. Es ergeben sich daher unten stehende Korrigenda. In der nächsten Auflage wird dieser Fehler korrigiert.

S./p. 61, Abb./fig. 74
Photo: **Zoom 77**
Vanunu M was hijacked in Rome ITL
1987

S./p. 89, Nr./no. 74
Photo: **Zoom 77**
Vanunu M was hijacked in Rome ITL/30.9.86/came to Rome
by BA Fly 504 – Vanunu M wurde in Rom ITL entführt/30.9.86/
kam nach Rom mit BA Flug 504
1987 IL Digital print
83,5 × 68 cm
Zoom 77

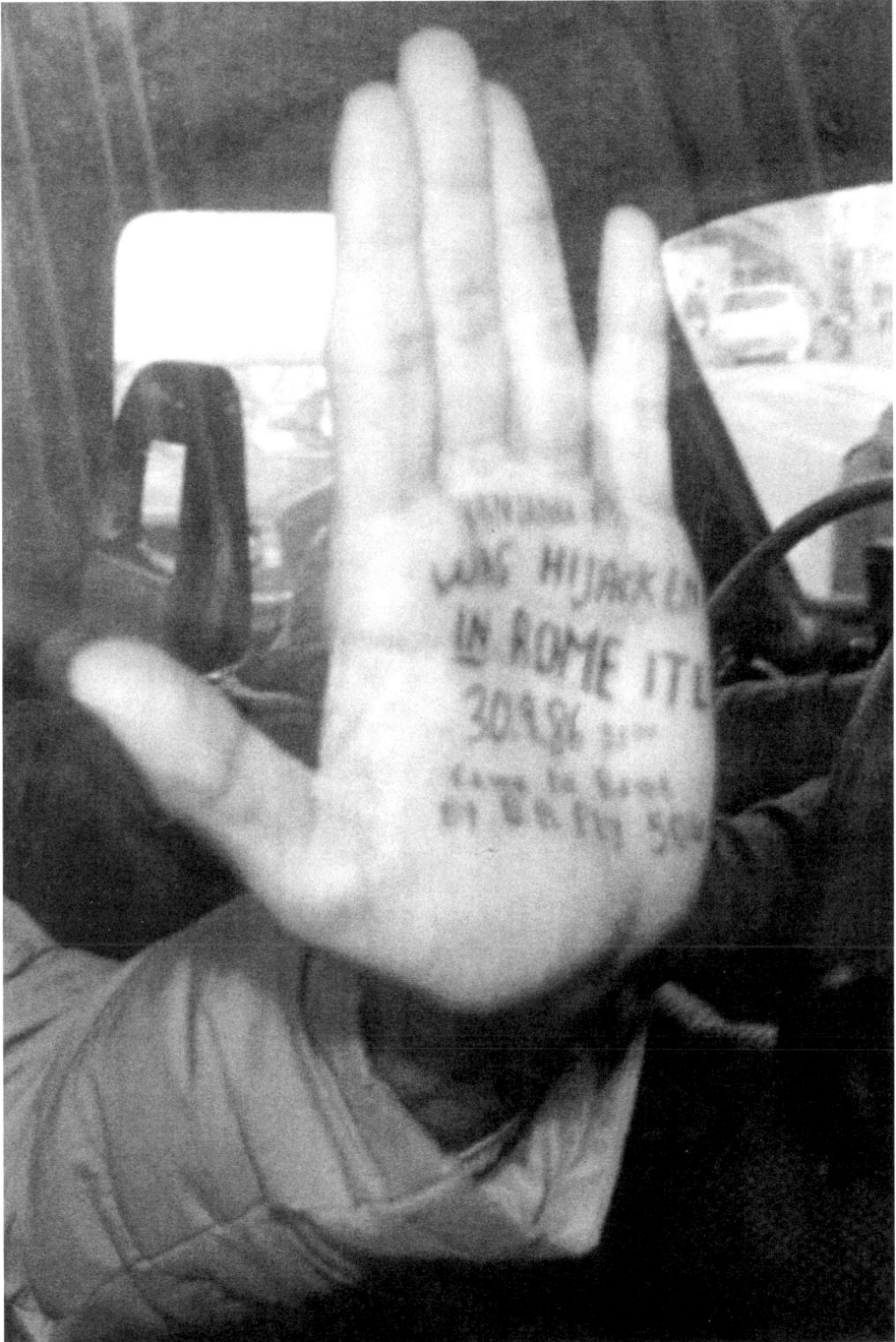

74 **David Tartakover**
Vanunu M was hijacked in Rome ITL
1987

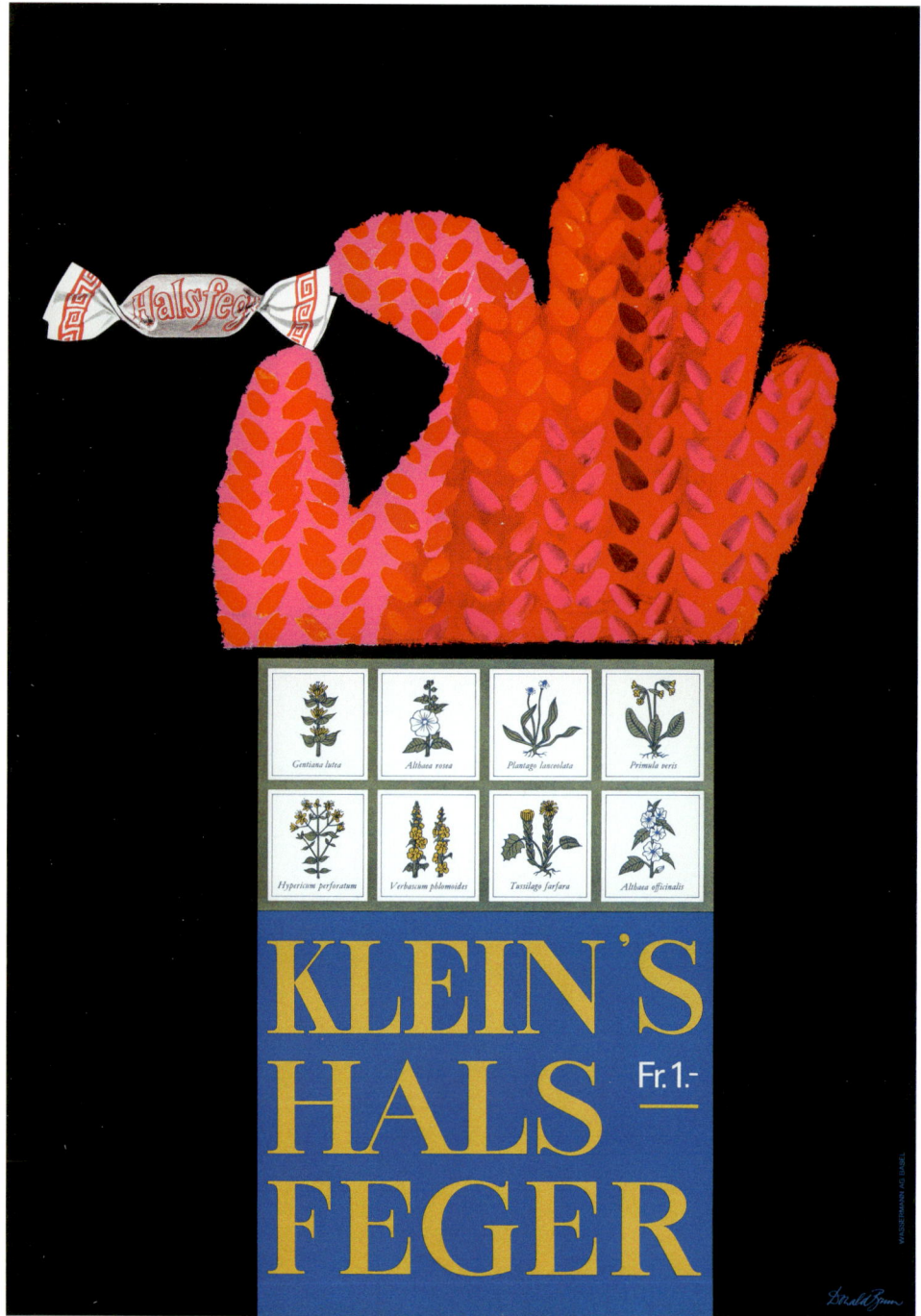

75 **Donald Brun**
Klein's Halsfeger
1967

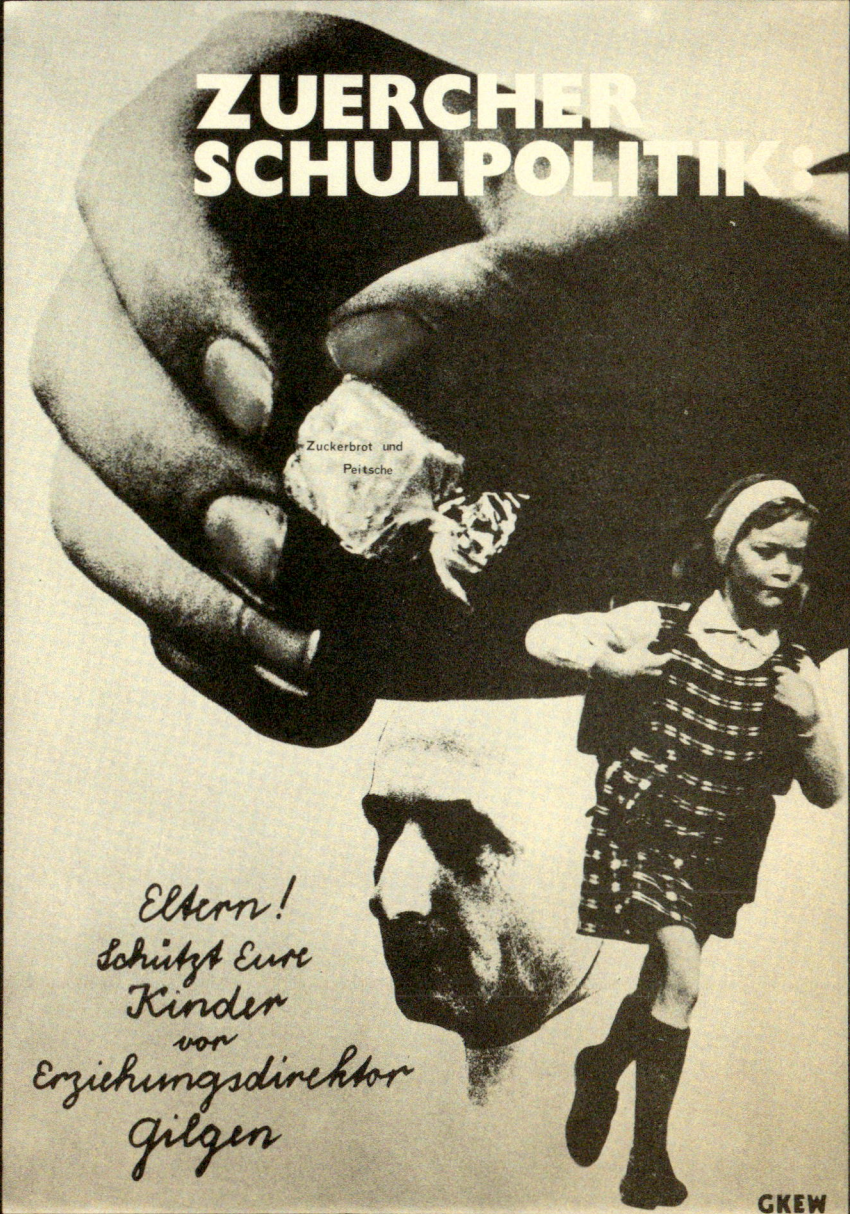

76 **anonym**
Zürcher Schulpolitik/Eltern! Schützt Eure Kinder
vor Erziehungsdirektor Gilgen
1975

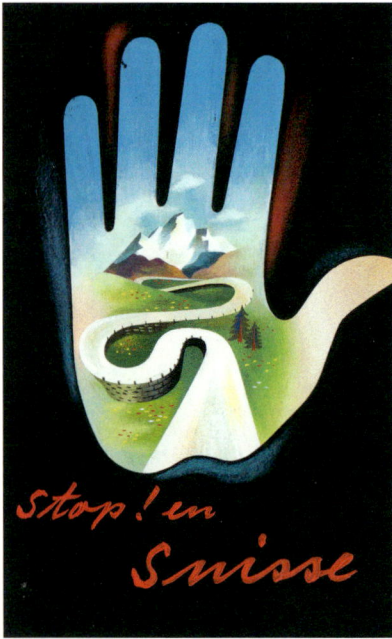

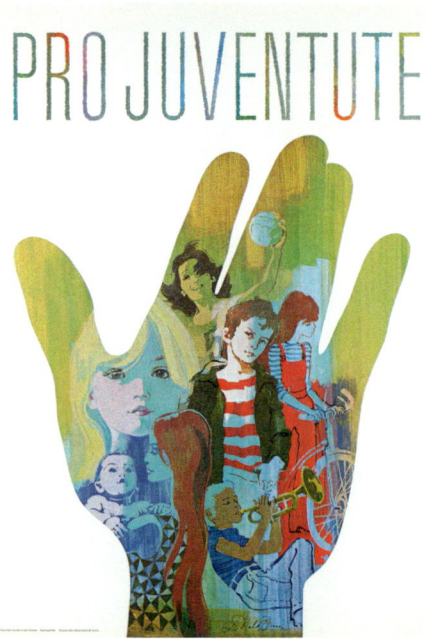

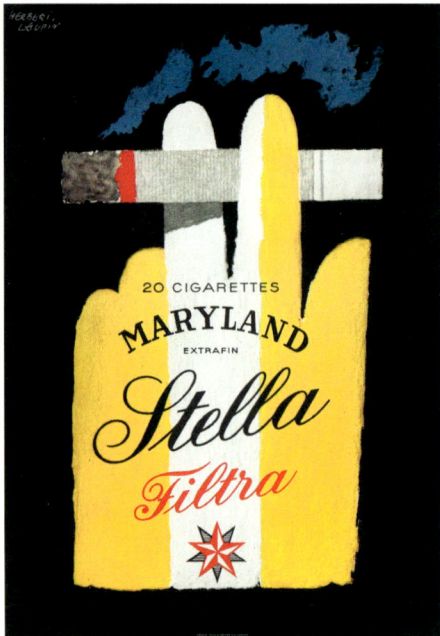

77 **anonym**
Stop! en Suisse
1937

78 **Herbert Leupin**
Maryland / Stella Filter
1956

79 **Donald Brun**
Pro Juventute
ca. 1955

80 **Herbert Leupin**
Tat … sachen!
1963

81 **Niklaus Stoecklin**
Vim putzt alles
1926

Entwurf: Michael Engelmann München

82 **Michael Engelmann**
Roth-Händle
1959

83 **Michael Engelmann**
Roth-Händle
1963

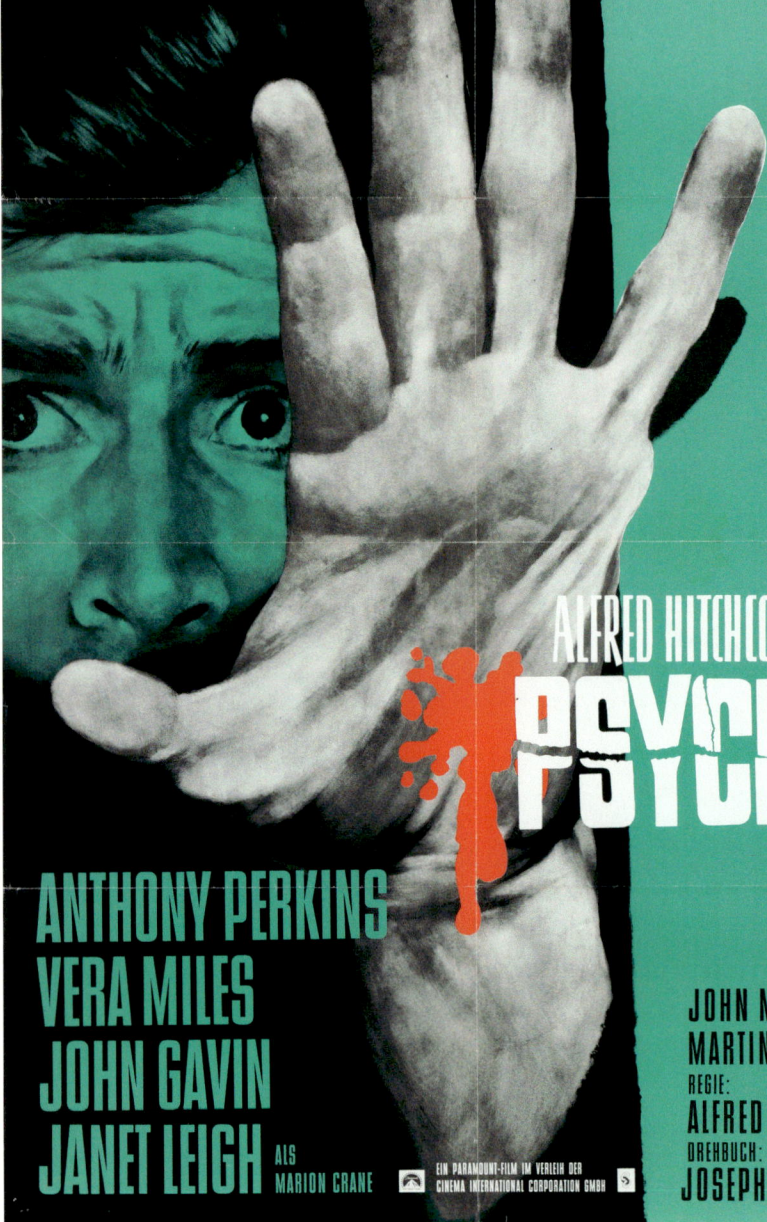

84 **Lutz Peltzer**
Alfred Hitchcock's Psycho
1960

ITALSKÝ FILM / DVA ÚSMĚVNÉ PŘÍBĚHY Z MANŽELSKÉHO ZÁKULISÍ / REŽIE: MARCO VICARIO
V HLAVNÍ ROLI MONICA VITTIOVÁ

PROMIŇ, ŽE JE TO MÁLO

85 **Karel Vaca**
Promiň, že je to málo
1984

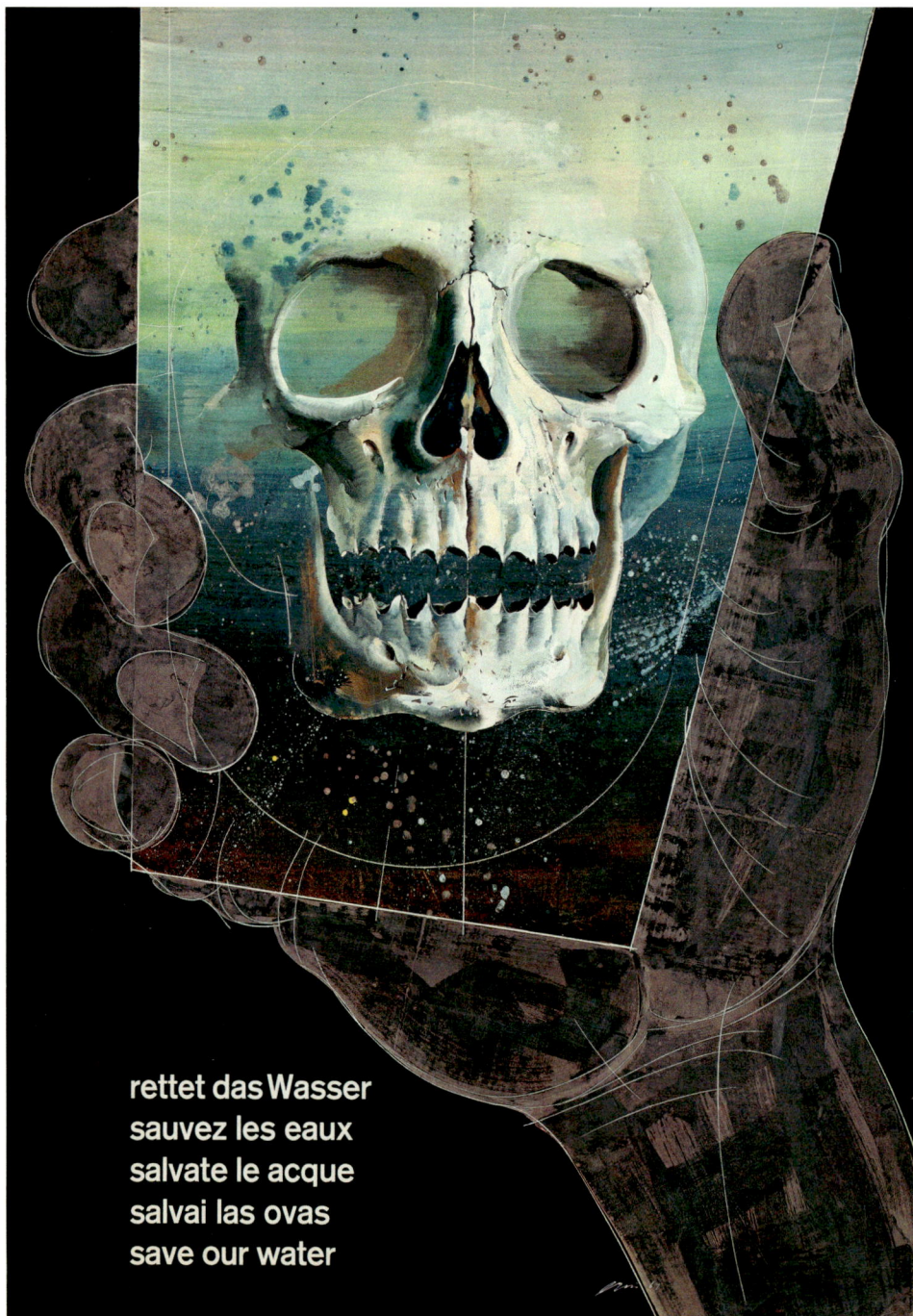

rettet das Wasser
sauvez les eaux
salvate le acque
salvai las ovas
save our water

86 **Hans Erni**
Rettet das Wasser
1961

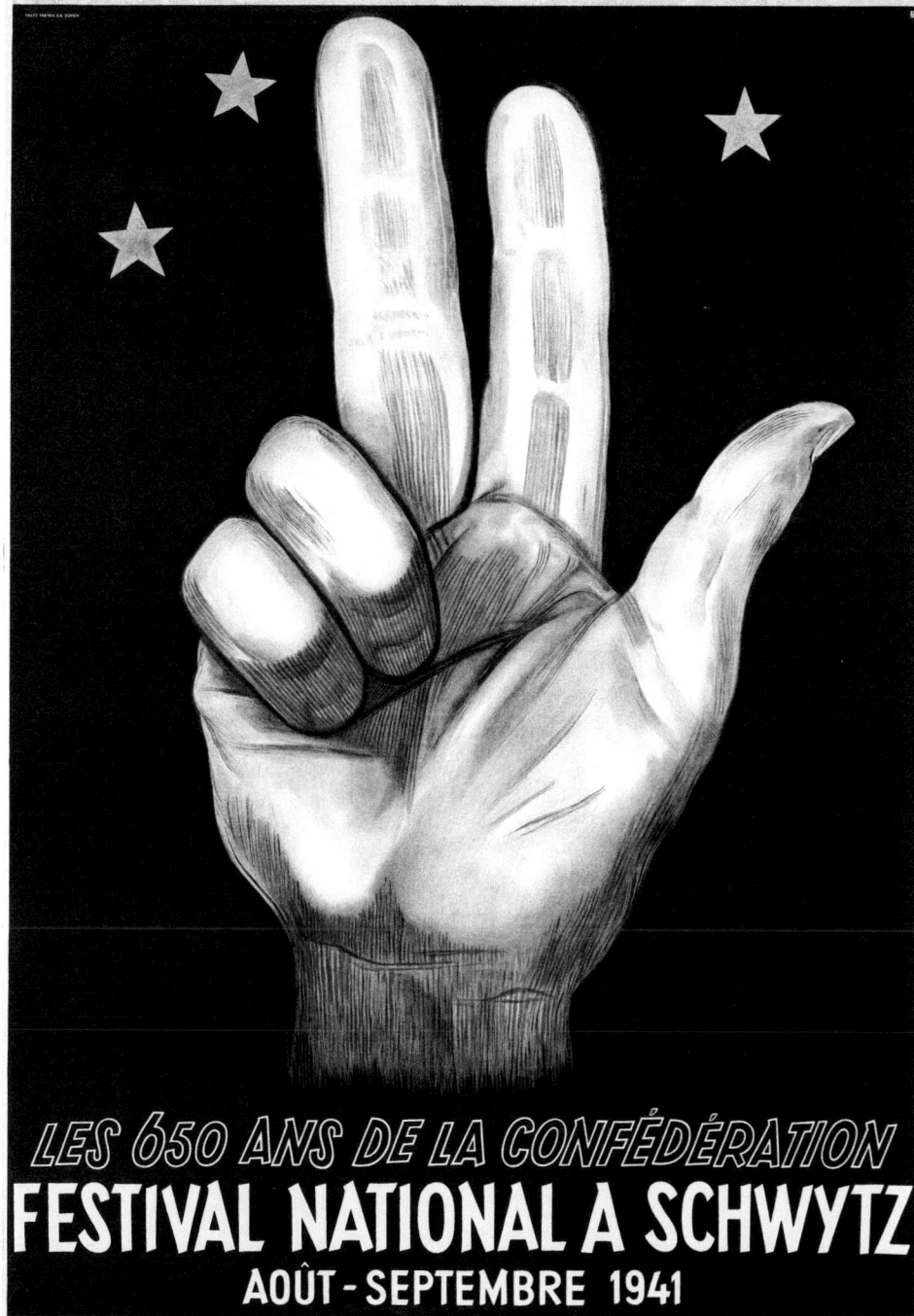

87 **Otto Baumberger**
Les 650 ans de la Confédération
1941

THE IMPACT OF THE HOLOCAUST AND GENOCIDE ON JEWS & CHRISTIANS

Remembering for the Future

An International Scholars Conference, Oxford, 10–13 July 1988
Public Conference, London, 15 July 1988

88 **Shigeo Fukuda**
Remembering for the Future
1988

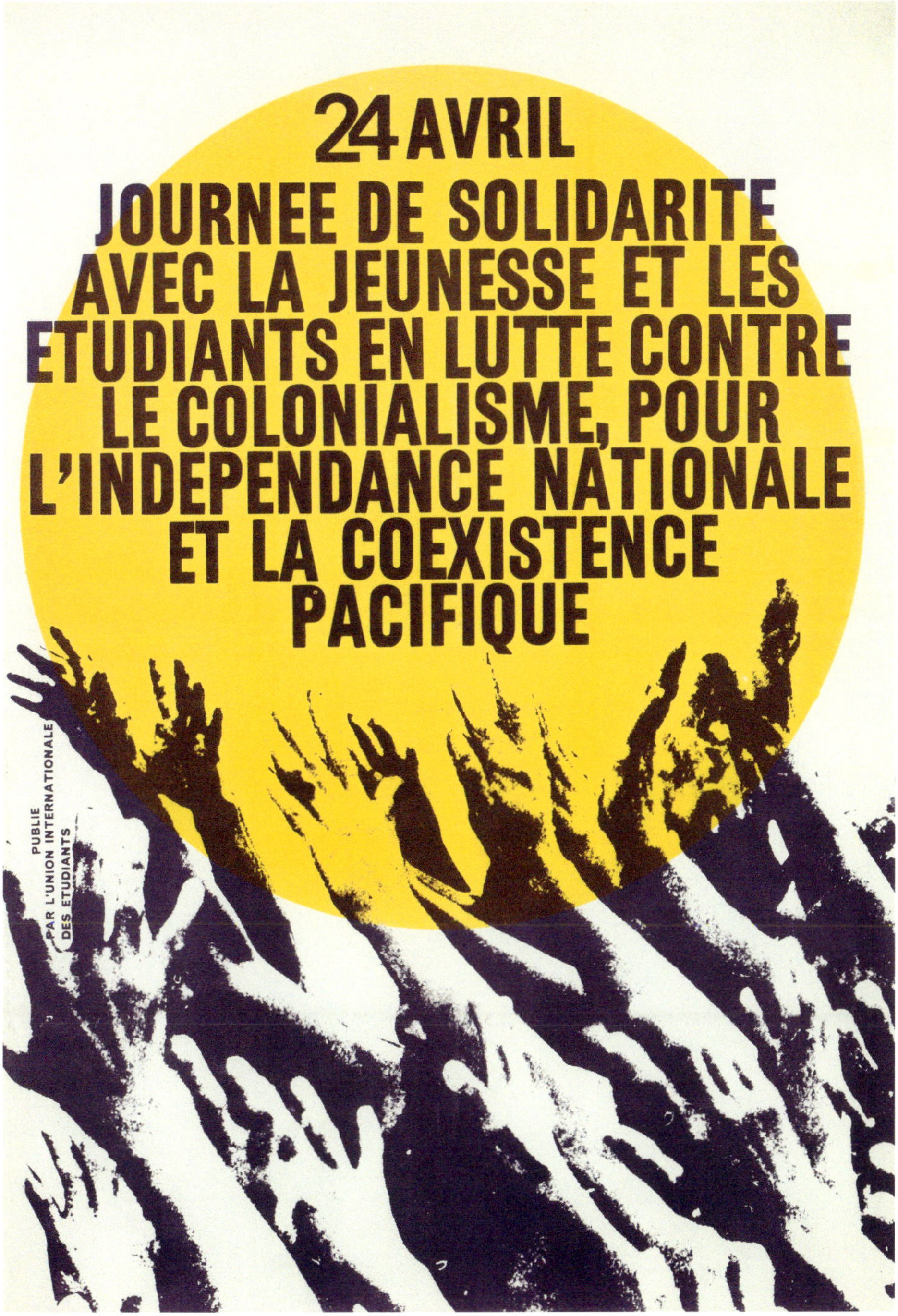

The poster text reads:

24 AVRIL
JOURNEE DE SOLIDARITE
AVEC LA JEUNESSE ET LES
ETUDIANTS EN LUTTE CONTRE
LE COLONIALISME, POUR
L'INDEPENDANCE NATIONALE
ET LA COEXISTENCE
PACIFIQUE

PUBLIE PAR L'UNION INTERNATIONALE DES ETUDIANTS

89 **anonym**
24 Avril Journée de solidarité
1972

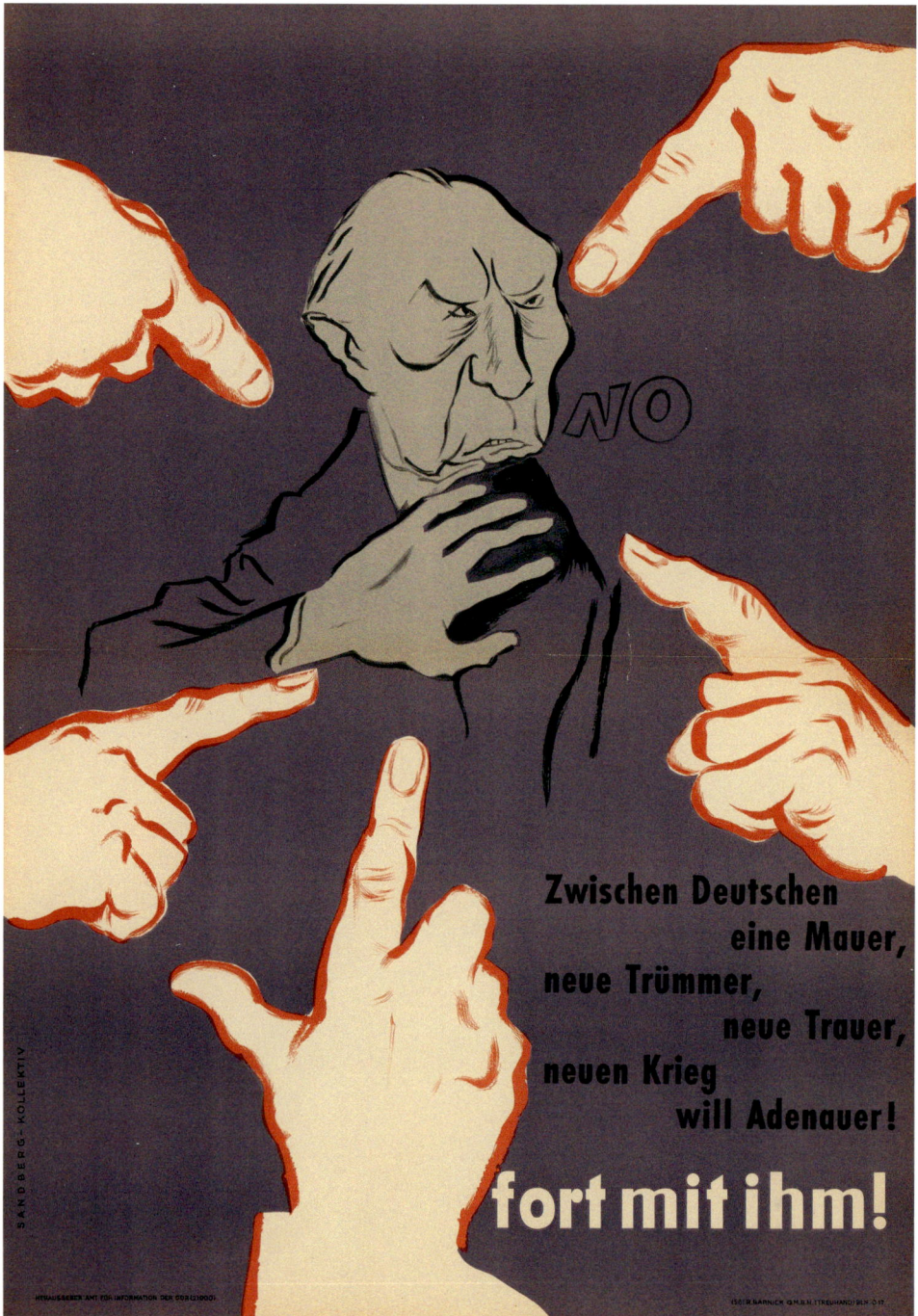

90 **Sandberg-Kollektiv**
Fort mit ihm!
ca. 1960

91 **anonym**
Frauenstimmrecht Nein
1959

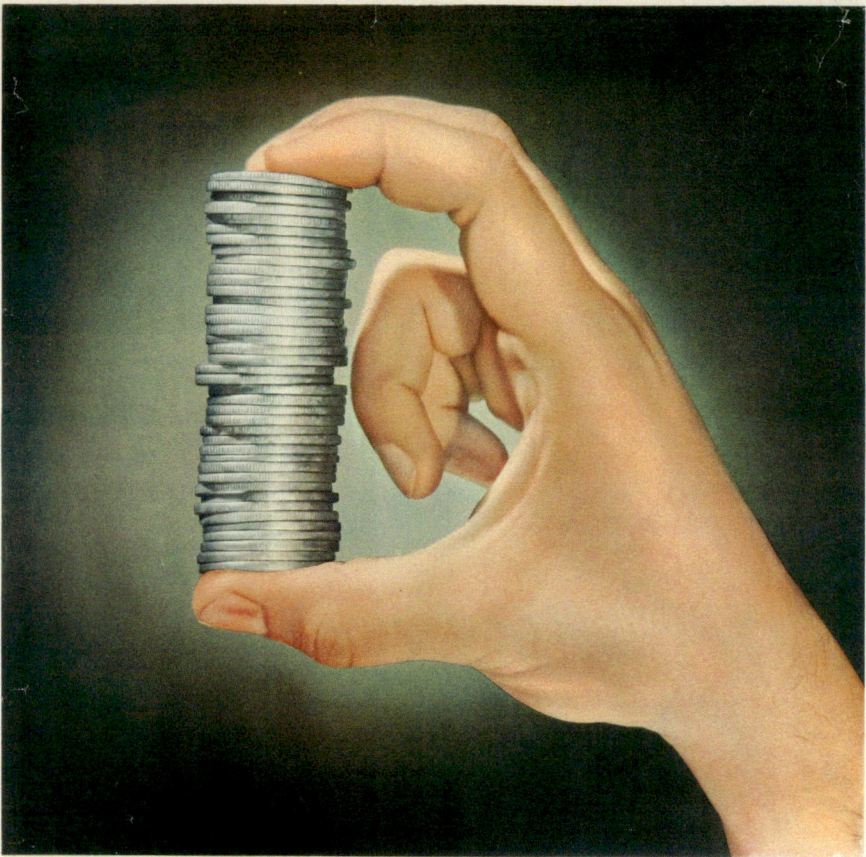

93 **Theyre Lee-Elliott**
Four Times the Number Carried
1936

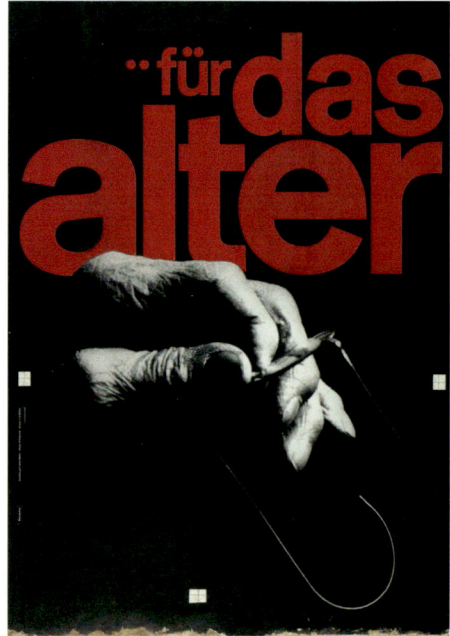

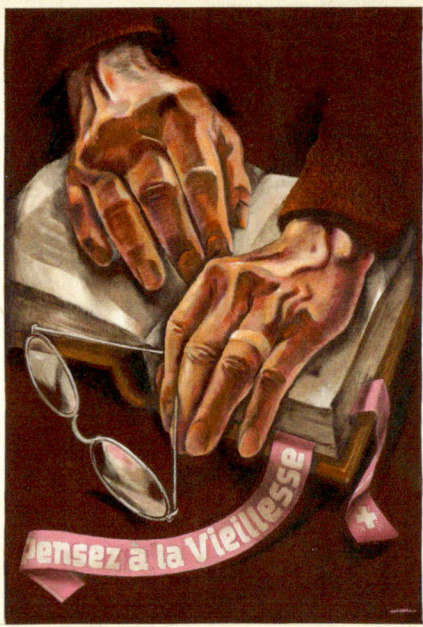

94 **Hans Aeschbach**
Sammlung Für das Alter
1947

95 **Ferdinand Maire**
Pensez à la vieillesse
ca. 1930

96 **Fridolin Müller**
Photo: Willi S. Eberle
Für das Alter
1964

97 **Karl Bickel**
Ja/Alter/Invalidität, 1925

78

98 Hans Rudolf Lauterburg
Photo: Fernand Rausser
Freiwillige Spende für das Alter
1963

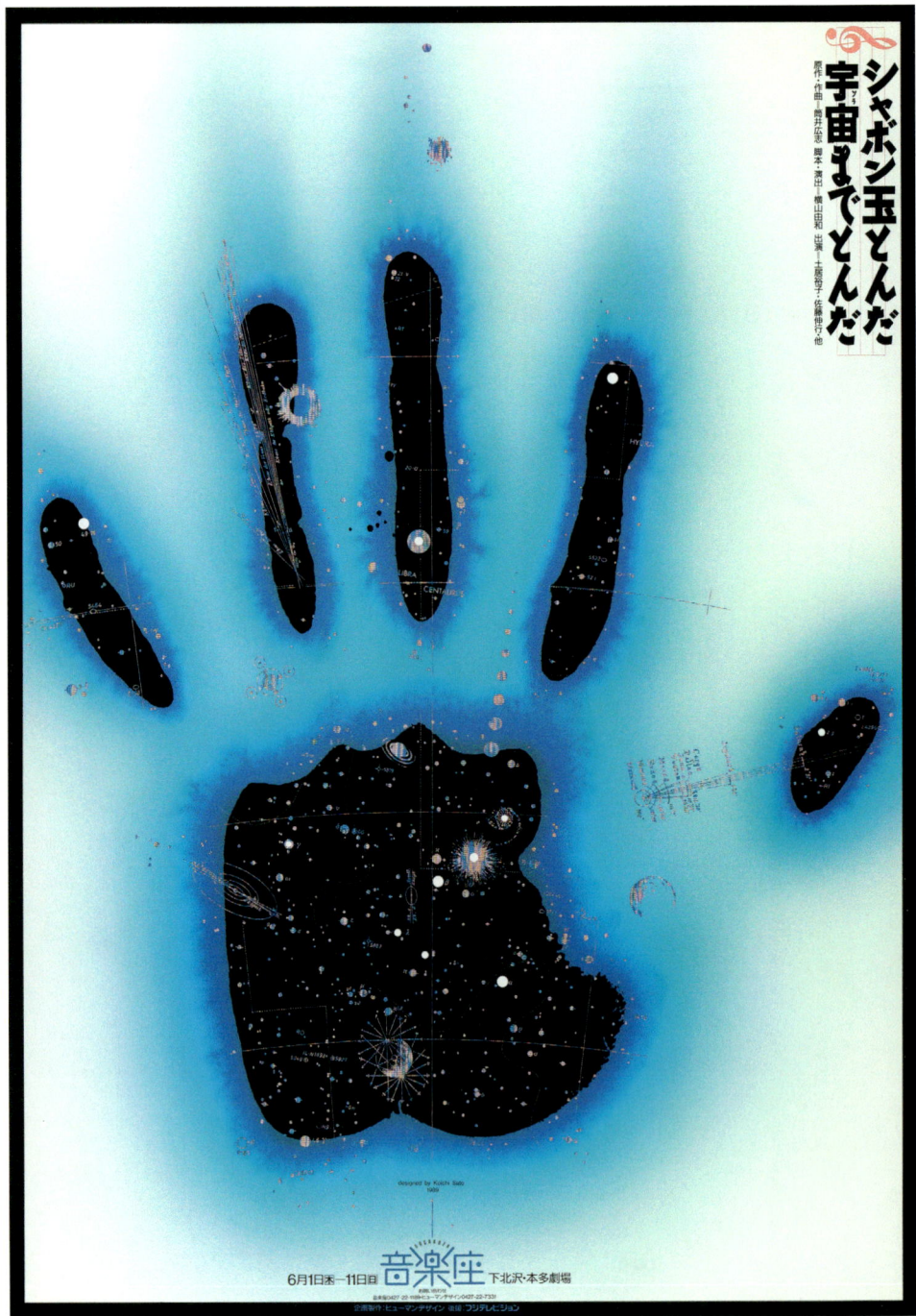

99 **Koichi Satō**
Ongakuza / Seifenblasen schwebten,
sie schwebten in den Weltraum
1989

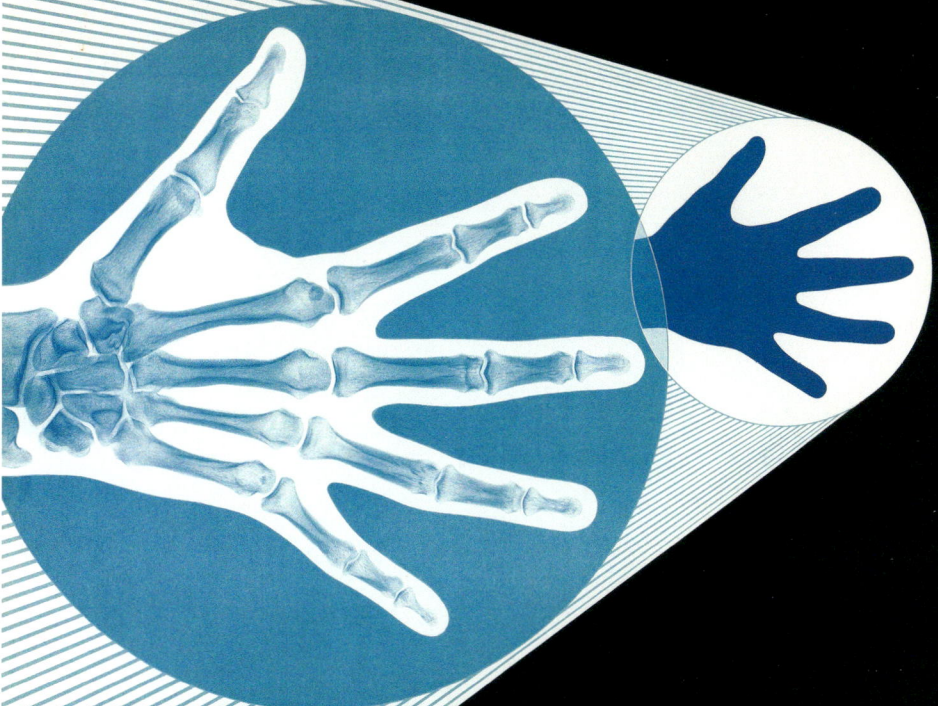

Käch / Druck: Gebr. Fretz AG. Zürich

Ausstellung des
IV. Internationalen
Radiologenkongresses
in Zürich

24. bis 29. Juli 1934

Ausstellungshalle :
Kunstgewerbemuseum

Ausstellungsleitung: A. Strelin, Präsident, Rämistrasse 7, Zürich

100 **Walter Käch**
Ausstellung des IV. Internationalen
Radiologenkongresses in Zürich
1934

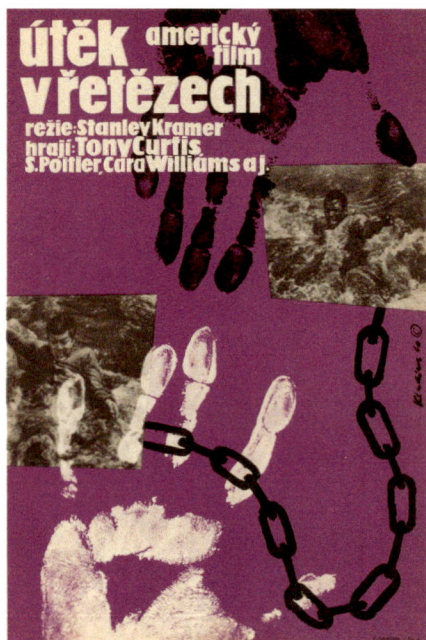

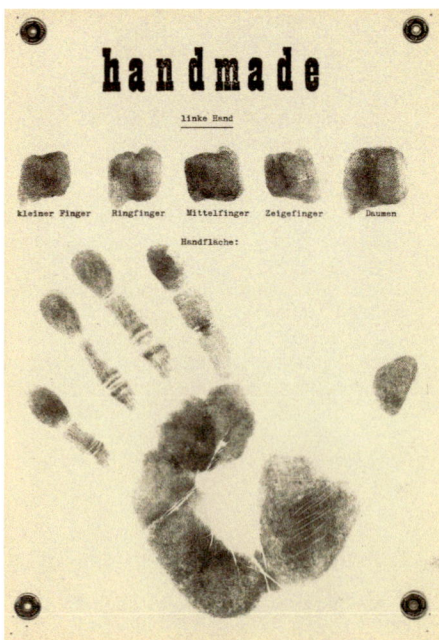

101 Eric Andersen
When we last met I should have said marriage
will be a disaster but death might be a success.
2013

102 anonym
Útěk v řetězech, 1960

103 M. Rojas
Pasaron los fascistas/… su huella
ca. 1937

104 Piär Amrein
Handmade
2005

105 **Pam Woll**
Equal opportunity/IBM
1992

106 **Pedro Yamashita**
No War/Don't Attack Iraq
2003

107 **Paul Brühwiler**
Plakate von Pabrü
2000

108 **Cornel Windlin**
Act Now
1992

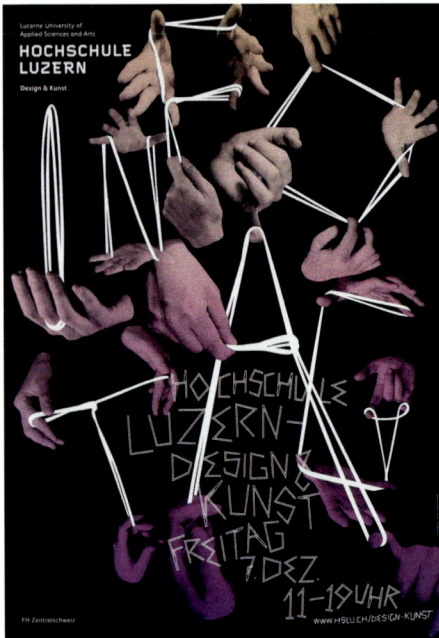

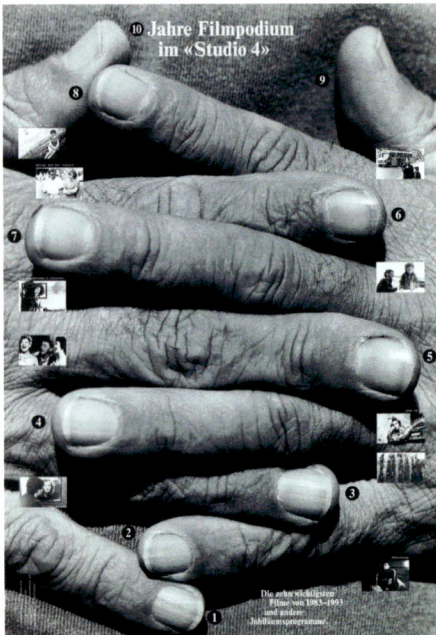

109 **Sabina Albanese**
Infotag Hochschule Luzern
2008

110 **Paul Brühwiler**
10 Jahre Filmpodium im «Studio 4»
1993

111 **Cornel Windlin / Gregor Huber**
Volpone
2010

112 **Mike Wells**
Levis 511 / Zip Fly
1995

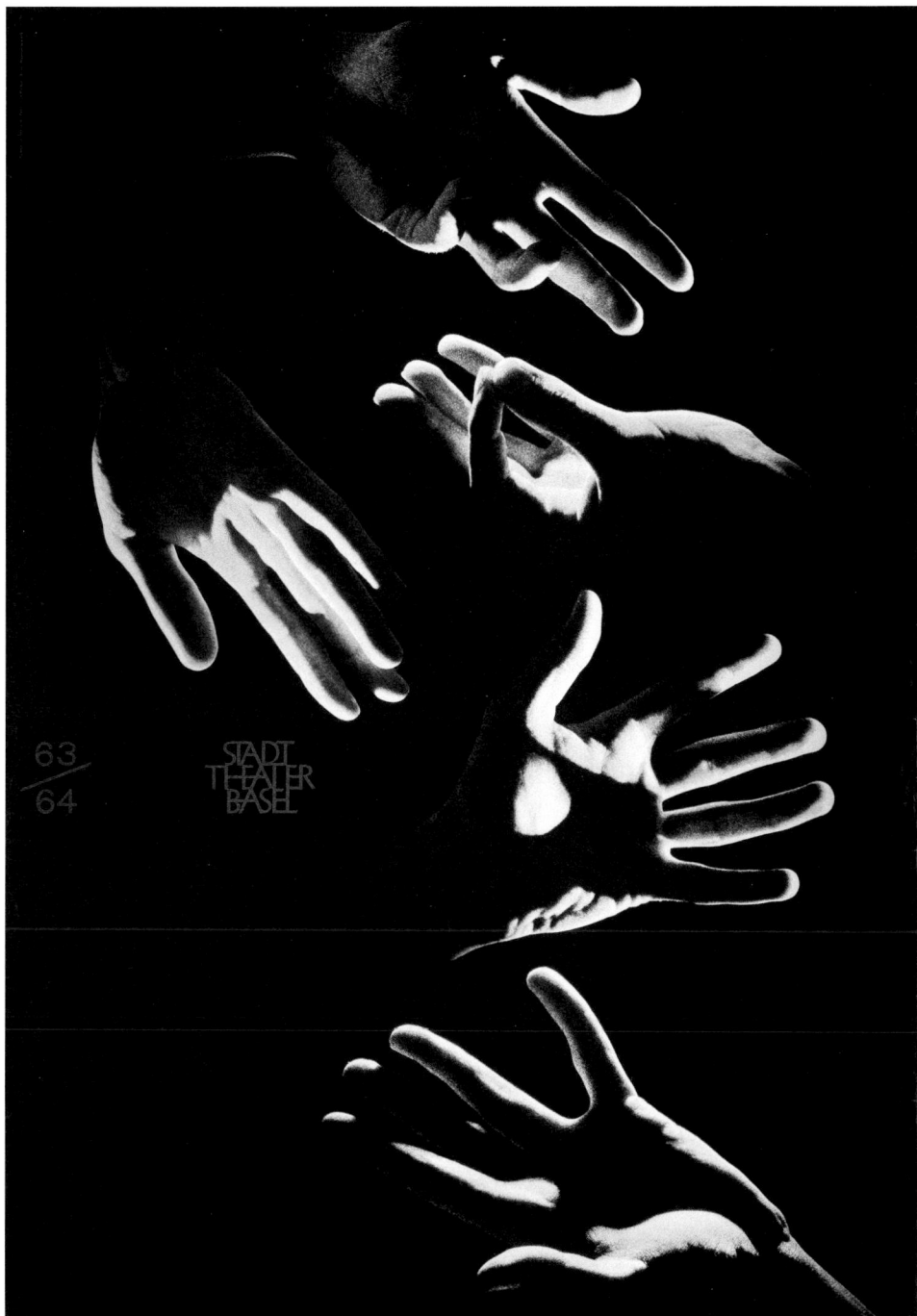

113 **Armin Hofmann**
Photo: Max Mathys
Stadttheater Basel 63/64
1963

Katalog

Alle abgebildeten Plakate stammen aus der
Plakatsammlung des Museum für Gestaltung Zürich.
Die Rechte (insbesondere Urheberrechte) liegen
bei den Autoren bzw. den Rechteinhabern.
© 2015, ProLitteris, Zürich: Eric Andersen 53, 54,
101; Otto Baumberger 87; Lester Beall 68, 69; Lucian
Bernhard 46; Paul Colin 31; John Heartfield 63;
Roy Lichtenstein 38; Richard Paul Lohse 60, 64;
Josef Müller-Brockmann 7; Martin Peikert 19; Niklaus
Stoecklin 81; Klaus Wittkugel 61.

Die Daten des Katalogs folgen den Rubriken Gestaltung,
Plakattext, Erscheinungsjahr, Erscheinungsland,
Drucktechnik, Format und Donationsnachweis. Dabei
gelten insbesondere folgende Regelungen:

Plakattext: Die beste Textwiedergabe bildet die Abbildung des Plakates selbst. Darum wird hier eine verein-
fachte Form wiedergegeben, welche nur die aussage-
kräftigen Textbestandteile berücksichtigt. Allfällige
Umstellungen dienen der Verständlichkeit. Das Zeichen / trennt inhaltliche Texteinheiten.

Erscheinungsland: Das Erscheinungsland wird mit dem
international gebräuchlichen ISO-Code angegeben.

Format: Die Angaben werden in der Abfolge
Höhe × Breite und in cm gemacht. Weil die Plakate
oft nicht exakt rechtwinklig geschnitten sind, werden
die Abmessungen auf halbe cm aufgerundet.

Donationsnachweis: Die Geschichte der Plakatsammlung geht auf das Jahr 1875 zurück. Angaben zur
Herkunft der Plakate sind in vielen Fällen nicht über-
liefert. Erst in jüngerer Zeit werden Donatoren von
Plakaten – Institutionen oder Einzelpersonen –
konsequent festgehalten und in Veröffentlichungen
namentlich publiziert.

Die Plakatgeschichte ist ein junges Forschungsgebiet –
verlässliche Hinweise sind rar. Jeder Hinweis und jede
Ergänzung sind willkommen:
sammlungen@museum-gestaltung.ch

Catalogue

All posters reproduced are from the Museum für
Gestaltung Zürich's Poster Collection. The copyrights
are held by the authors, and their legal successors.
© 2015, ProLitteris, Zürich: Eric Andersen 53, 54,
101; Otto Baumberger 87; Lester Beall 68, 69; Lucian
Bernhard 46; Paul Colin 31; John Heartfield 63;
Roy Lichtenstein 38; Richard Paul Lohse 60, 64;
Josef Mülller-Brockmann 7; Martin Peikert 19; Niklaus
Stoecklin 81; Klaus Wittkugel 61.

The data listed in the catalogue is broken down into
the following sections: designer, poster title and/or text,
year and country of first appearance, printing technique,
size, and donor. In particular, the following rules have
been applied:

Poster text: The poster itself provides the best version
of the text, and thus a simplified form is used which
provides only the most meaningful elements. Any
rearrangements that have been made are for purposes
of intelligibility. A slash mark separates textual units
by content.

Country of first appearance: The country of first
appearance is identified by the internationally accepted
ISO code.

Format: The dimensions are given in centimeters as
height × width. Because posters are often not cut exactly
at right angles, the dimensions are rounded off to the
half centimeter.

Donor: The history of the Poster Collection goes back
to 1875. In many cases, we lack specific information
concerning the sources of posters in the collection.
Only recently have institutional or individual contributors
of posters been recorded consistently and specified
in our publications.

The history of posters is a recent field of research—
reliable information is rare. Any further references or
additional material are welcome:
sammlungen@museum-gestaltung.ch

1 Cornel Windlin (1964–)/
Gregor Huber (1978–)
Schauspielhaus Zürich/Saison 2010/11
2010 CH Siebdruck – Screenprint
132 × 97 cm
Donation Cornel Windlin

2 anonym
La pègre au pouvoir – Die Unterwelt
an die Macht – Gangsters Rule
the Roost
1968 FR Siebdruck – Screenprint
67 × 51 cm

3 Asela Maria Pérez (1934–)
Jornada internacional de solidaridad
con America Latina – Internationale
Solidaritätswoche mit Lateinamerika –
International Week of Solidarity with
Latin America
1968 CU Offset 54,5 × 33 cm

4 Faydherbe/De Vringer
Ben Faydherbe (1958–)/
Wout De Vringer (1959–)
[ohne Text – no text]
2008 NL Siebdruck – Screenprint
84,5 × 59,5 cm
Donation Faydherbe/De Vringer

5 Adolphe Mouron Cassandre
(1901–1968)
Thomson/La main-d'œuvre électro
domestique – Thomson/Die Arbeits-
kraft für Heimelektronik – Thomson/
Consumer Electronics Working for You
1931 FR Lithografie – Lithograph
119 × 80 cm

6 Uwe Loesch (1943–)
Ich bin Rahmen für Handlung/Ich bin
Kunstdruck für Druckkunst/Ikonolux
von Zanders – I Frame Action/
I Am an Art Print for Print Art/
Ikonolux by Zanders
1986 DE Offset 135 × 97 cm
Donation Uwe Loesch

7 Josef Müller-Brockmann (1914–1996)
Photo: René Burri (1933–2014)
Das freundliche Handzeichen schützt
vor Unfällen – A Friendly Hand Signal
Prevents Accidents
1955 CH Offset 127 × 90 cm

8 Percy Wenger (zugeschrieben –
attributed to, 1918–1992)
Vin Vaudois/Vin doré – Waadtländer
Wein/Goldener Wein – Vaud Wine/
Golden Wine
1946 CH Gouache, Ölkreide –
Gouache, wax oil crayon 127 × 90 cm
Plakatentwurf – Poster design
Donation Percy Wenger

9 Ernst Keller (1891–1968)
Kunstgewerbemuseum Zürich/Ausstel-
lungen Walter Gropius/Rationelle
Bebauungsweisen – Kunstgewerbemuseum Zürich/Walter Gropius Exhibi-
tions/Rational Construction Methods
1931 CH Hochdruck – Letterpress
printing 127 × 90 cm

10 Edi Hauri (1911–1988)
Geroba Tabletten/Gegen Husten –
Geroba Tablets/Stop Coughs
1936 CH Lithografie – Lithograph
128 × 90 cm

11 Hannes Portmann (1927–2007)
Photo: Willi S. Eberle (1931–)
Vivi-Kola/Mit Eglisauer Mineralwasser
– Vivi-Kola/With Eglisau Mineral Water
1957 CH Lithografie – Lithograph
128 × 90,5 cm

12 Adolphe Mouron Cassandre
(1901–1968)
Pacific
1935 CH Lithografie – Lithograph
128 × 90 cm

13 Hermann Eidenbenz (1902–1993)
Zweifel Süssmost ist gesund –
Zweifel Apple Juice is healthy
1951 CH Lithografie – Lithograph
128,5 × 90,5 cm

14 Charles Kuhn (1903–1999)
Téléphone international – Telefonie
international – International Telephone
1930 CH Lithografie – Lithograph
127 × 90 cm

15 Hans Neuburg (1904–1983)
Das Zeichen für handwerkliche
Massarbeit/Centralverband Schweiz/
Schneidermeister – The Mark of
Craftsmanship/Central Association of
Swiss Master Tailors
1950 CH Lithografie – Lithograph
128 × 90,5 cm

16 anonym
Olivetti Lexikon Elettrica
1961 IT Offset 70 × 50 cm

17 Heinz Waibl (1931–)
La scarpa Gasparotto/Elegante/
Robusta/Comoda – Der Gasparotto-
Schuh/Elegant/Robust/Bequem –
Gasparotto Shoes/Elegant/Robust/
Comfortable
1959 IT Offset 68 × 46,5 cm

18 Walter Bangerter (1907–1986)/
Klaus Fischer
Bigla Stahlmöbel/Büro-Organi-
sationen/Oberholzer Zürich –
Bigla Steel Furnishings/Office
Organizations/Oberholzer Zurich
1954 CH Hochdruck – Letterpress
printing 128 × 90,5 cm

19 Martin Peikert (1901–1975)
Paillard Radio
1937 CH Lithografie –
Lithograph 128 × 90,5 cm
Donation Suzanne Marie
Peikert-Borboën

20 Heinrich Steiner (1906–1983)
Photo: Ernst Albrecht Heiniger
(1909–1993)
Téléphonez – Telefoniert –
Telephone
1939 CH Tiefdruck – Gravure print
127,5 × 89,5 cm

21 Arno Löffler
Trinkt mehr Milch! – Drink More
Milk!
1937 AT Offset 60,5 × 47 cm

22 Melchior Annen (1868–1954)
Tungsram D
1937 CH Lithografie – Lithograph
127 × 90 cm

23 Willi Günthart-Maag (1915–1997)
Photo: Ernst Albrecht Heiniger
(1909–1993)
Per il pane di domani/Legge sull'
agricoltura, votate sí – Für das
Brot von morgen/Landwirtschafts-
gesetz, stimmt ja – For
Tomorrow's Bread/Vote Yes to
the Agriculture Bill
1952 CH Offset 59 × 41 cm
Donation Archiv für Agrargeschichte,
AFA, Zollikofen

24 Viktor Rutz (1913–2008)
Floralp Butter am besten –
Floralp, the Best of Butter
1939 CH Lithografie – Lithograph
127 × 90 cm

25 April Greiman (1948–)
Summer Programs 1991/Architec-
ture: Education and Instruction/
Southern California Institute of
Architecture – Sommerprogramm
1991/Architektur: Ausbildung und
Lehre/Southern California Institute
of Architecture
1991 US Offset 127 × 101,5 cm

26 Frédéric Henri Kay Henrion
(1914–1990)
Design at Home – Design zu Hause
1949 GB Lithografie – Lithograph
76 × 49 cm

27 El' Lisickij (1880–1941)
Pelican Drawing Ink.
1925 GB Lithografie – Lithograph
32,5 × 44,5 cm

28 Otl Aicher (1922–1991)
Wann endlich Europa? – Europe
At Last?
1951 DE Offset 83 × 41,5 cm

29 Otl Aicher (1922–1991)
Ein Jahrhundert bittet um Frieden –
A Century Calls for Peace
1948 DE Offset 83 × 42 cm

30 Otl Aicher (1922–1991)
Weltwirtschaft – World Economy
1948 DE Offset 81,5 × 41 cm

31 Paul Colin (1892–1985)
Gham-bō …/Seul
1930 FR Lithografie – Lithograph
58 × 38,5 cm

32 Otl Aicher (1922–1991)
Der europäische Familienzwist –
Strife in the European Family
1951 DE Siebdruck – Screenprint
40,5 × 41,5 cm

33 anonym
Stadtpolizei Zürich/Zentrale
Beratungsstelle für Verbrechens-
Verhütung – Zurich Municipal Police/
Central Crime Prevention Advice
Center
1967 CH Offset 127 × 90 cm

34 Viktor Rutz (1913–2008)
Wer rechnet, kauft im Globus –
Smart Shoppers Save at Globus
1937 CH Lithografie – Lithograph
127 × 90 cm

35 Robert Siebold
Vorsicht – Watch Out
ca. 1987 CH Siebdruck – Screenprint
128 × 90 cm
Donation Stadtpolizei Zürich

36 anonym
Razoblacim i uničtožim provokatorov i
rasprostranitelej paničeskich sluchov –
Wir entlarven und liquidieren die
Provokateure und Verbreiter von Panik-
gerüchten – We Unmask and Liquidate
Agents Provocateurs and Panic-
mongers
1941 SU Offset 57 × 36 cm

37 Atelier Populaire
Le vote ne change rien/La lutte
continue – Die Wahlen ändern nichts/
Der Kampf geht weiter –
The Vote Changes Nothing/
The Struggle Goes On
1968 FR Siebdruck – Screenprint
95,5 × 70 cm

38 Roy Lichtenstein (1923–1997)
Amerikansk Pop-konst/Moderna
Museet – Amerikanische Pop
Art/Moderna Museet – American Pop
Art/Moderna Museet
1965 SE Siebdruck – Screenprint
90,5 × 61 cm

39 Shigeo Fukuda (1932–2009)
Shigeo Fukuda/The Ginza Tokyo
1979 JP Siebdruck – Screenprint
103 × 73 cm
Donation DNP Foundation for Cultural
Promotion, Tokio und Shizuko Fukuda

40 Karl Gerstner (1930–)
Auch Du bist liberal – You Too Are
Liberal
1956 CH Offset 127 × 90 cm

41 Shigeo Fukuda (1932–2009)
Shigeo Fukuda/Illustrick
1990 JP Offset 103 × 73 cm
Donation DNP Foundation für Cultural
Promotion, Tokio und Shizuko Fukuda

42 Bernhard Lüthi
Für Ihre Sicherheit nur dieses
Überkleid – For Your Safety,
Only This Overall Will Do
ca. 1966 CH Offset 127 × 90 cm

43 Digby Wills Ltd.
The new ‹Zebra› crossings/Respect
them/Use them – Die neuen Zebra-
streifen/Respektiert sie/Nutzt sie
1950 GB Offset 76 × 50 cm

44 Hans Hartmann (1913–1991)
Handzeichen schaffen Klarheit –
A Hand Signal Makes Things Clear
1936 CH Offset 127 × 90 cm

45 C. E. Gogler
Confiscation de la propriété/Non –
Konfiszierung des Privateigen-
tums/Nein – Confiscation of Private
Property/No
1922 CH Lithografie – Lithograph
127 × 90 cm

46 Lucian Bernhard (1883–1972)
Tretet ein in den Grenzschutz Ost!
Schützt die Heimat gegen Bolsche-
wismus! Meldung beim nächsten
Garnison- oder Bezirks-Kommando. –
Enlist in the Eastern Border Defense
Force! Protect Our Homeland Against
Bolshevism! Register at the Closest
Garrison or District Headquarters.
1919 DE Lithografie – Lithograph
94,5 × 72 cm

47 Fritz Rosen (1890–1980)
Starke Hand – rettet das Land –
A Strong Hand – Saves the Land
ca. 1932 DE Lithografie – Lithograph
120 × 86,5 cm

48 Michail Michajlovič Čeremnych
(1890–1962)
Pravil'no v poslovice skazano:
«Vse popy odnim mirom mazany»!
Vse oni propovedujut bez isključenija
čuždoe kommunizmu «učenie».
Ne poddavajtes' popovs komu
obmanu. Osvoboždajtes' ot religioz-
nogo durmana! – Das Sprichwort
sagt es richtig: «Alle Popen sind vom
gleichen Schlag!» Ohne Ausnahme
predigen sie alle die dem Kommu-
nismus fremde «Lehre». Lasst euch
von den Popen nicht hinters Licht
führen. Befreit euch aus der reli-
giösen Betäubung! – "Papists are
all the same!" They preach an anti-
Communist "doctrine." Don't let the
papists fool you! Break free of
religious brainwashing!
1938 SU Offset 87,5 × 55 cm

49 Atelier Populaire
Université Populaire/Été 68 –
Volksuniversität/Sommer 68 –
People's University/Summer 68
1968 FR Siebdruck – Screenprint
76 × 64 cm

50 Peter von Arx (1937–)/
Peter Olpe (1949–)
Kunst und Politik/Kunsthalle Basel –
Art and Politics/Kunsthalle Basel
1971 CH Offset 128 × 90,5 cm

51 anonym
Heraus zum 1. Mai/POCH Progressive Organisation – All out on May 1/
POCH Progressive Organization
1975 CH Siebdruck – Screenprint
127 × 90 cm

52 Gregor Huber (1978–)/
Ivan Sterzinger (1979–)
Talk to the Hand/Helmhaus Zürich
2013 CH Xerox, Siebdruck –
Screenprint 128,5 × 89,5 cm
Donation Helmhaus Zürich

53 Eric Andersen (1981–)
1. Mai 2014/Mit einer geballten
Faust kann man keinen Händedruck
wechseln. – May 1, 2014/You can't
shake hands with a clenched fist.
2014 CH Siebdruck – Screenprint
100 × 70 cm
Donation Eric Andersen

54 Eric Andersen (1981–)
1. Mai 2014/Mit einer geballten
Faust kann man keinen Händedruck
wechseln. – May 1, 2014/You can't
shake hands with a clenched fist.
2014 CH Siebdruck – Screenprint
100 × 70 cm
Donation Eric Andersen

55 Happypets Products
Cédric Henny (1971–)/Patrick Monnier
(1974–)/Violène Pont (1974–)
Ubu Roi/Théâtre du Moulin-Neuf/
Aigle
2004 CH Offset 55 × 40 cm
Donation Happypets Products

56 Happypets Products
Cédric Henny (1971–)/Patrick Monnier
(1974–)/Violène Pont (1974–)
Les frères normal/Théâtre du
Moulin-Neuf/Aigle
2004 CH Offset 55 × 40 cm
Donation Happypets Products

57 Ruedi Wyss (1949–)
Eine japanische Nacht/Jazz Now
Bern – A Japanese Evening/
Jazz Now Bern
1984 CH Offset 59,5 × 42,5 cm
Donation Ruedi Wyss

58 Lukas Zimmermann (1977–)
[ohne Text – no text]
2002 CH Xerox 59,5 × 42 cm
Donation Lukas Zimmermann

59 Flag
Bastien Aubry (1974–)/Dimitri
Broquard (1969–)
Theater hat Nebenwirkungen/
Stadttheater Bern – Theater Has
Side-effects/Stadttheater Bern
2004 CH Siebdruck – Screenprint
128 × 89,5 cm
Donation Flag

60 Richard Paul Lohse (1902–1988)
Photo: Ernst Albrecht Heiniger
(1909–1993)
Deine Zeitung – das Volksrecht –
Your Newspaper – das Volksrecht
1942 CH Tiefdruck – Gravure print
128 × 90,5 cm

61 Klaus Wittkugel (1910–1985)
Arbeiter! In die Partei der Arbeiter! –
Workers! Join the Workers' Party!
1956 DD Offset 84 × 59,5 cm

62 Gustav Gustavovič Klucis
(1895–1938)
Vypolnim plan velikich rabot –
Erfüllen wir den Plan der grossen
Arbeiten – Let's Fulfill the Plan of
Great Works
1930 SU Lithografie – Lithograph
118 × 83 cm

63 John Heartfield (1891–1968)
5 Finger hat die Hand/Mit 5 packst
Du den Feind! Wählt Liste 5/
Kommunistische Partei! –
5 Fingers Has the Hand/With 5 You
Can Grab the Enemy! Vote List
5/Communist Party!
1928, Nachdruck – Reprint 1976 DD
Tiefdruck – Gravure print 64 × 48 cm

64 Richard Paul Lohse (1902–1988)
Helft uns helfen/Schweiz. Winterhilfe
– Help Us to Help/Swiss Winter Aid
1940 CH Tiefdruck – Gravure print
127 × 90 cm

65 Oliviero Toscani (1942–)
United Colors of Benetton
1990 IT Offset 30 × 42 cm

66 Advico Young & Rubicam AG
René Schmid
Photo: Karl Keller
Eine Versicherungspolice ist …/
… eine Sicherheit – An Insurance
Policy Offers …/… Security
1966 CH Offset 127 × 90 cm

67 Heidi Franceschini
Danke. Helvetas – Thank You, Helvetas
ca. 1991 CH Offset 128 × 90,5 cm

68 Lester Beall (1903–1969)
Slums Breed Crime/United States
Housing Authority – Slums vermehren
Verbrechen/United States Housing
Authority
1941 US Lithografie – Lithograph
110 × 84 cm

69 Lester Beall (1903–1969)
Cross out Slums/USHA –
Vernichtet Slums/USHA
1941 US Lithografie – Lithograph
110 × 84 cm

70 Les Graphistes Associés
Liens de familles/La famille, à quoi
ça sert?/Musée national des arts et
traditions populaires – Familienbande/
Die Familie, wozu ist sie gut?/Musée
national des arts et traditions populaires – Family Ties/What's the Point
of the Family?/Musée national des
arts et traditions populaires
1991 FR Offset 60 × 40 cm
Donation Les Graphistes Associés

71 DNS-Transport
Ueli Kleeb (1964–)/Caroline Lötscher
(1974–)
7 Tage Auferstehen in den 17 Zuger
Pfarreien/Zuger Dekanat – 7 Days of
Resurrection in the 17 Zug Parishes/
Zug Deanery
2006 CH Siebdruck – Screenprint
128 × 90 cm
Donation DNS-Transport

72 DNS-Transport
Ueli Kleeb (1964–)/Caroline
Lötscher (1974–)
Pfarrei St. Jakobus der Ältere/Cham
2006 CH Siebdruck – Screenprint
128 × 90 cm
Donation DNS-Transport

73 Paula Troxler (1981–)
Integral gibt ein Fest im Anker –
Integral's Throwing a Party at Anker
2007 CH Siebdruck – Screenprint
128 × 91 cm
Donation Paula Troxler

74 David Tartakover (1944–)
Vanunu M was hijacked in Rome
ITL/30.9.86/came to Rome by BA
Fly 504 – Vanunu M wurde in
Rom ITL entführt/30.9.86/Kam
nach Rom mit BA Flug 504
1987 IL Digitaldruck – Digital print
98,5 × 68 cm
Donation David Tartakover

75 Donald Brun (1909–1999)
Klein's Halsfeger – Klein's
Halsfeger [cough drops]
1967 CH Offset 127 × 90 cm

76 anonym
Zürcher Schulpolitik/Eltern!
Schützt Eure Kinder vor Erziehungs-
direktor Gilgen – Zurich School
Politics/Parents! Protect
Your Children from Director of
Education Gilgen
1975 CH Offset 30 × 21 cm

77 anonym
Stop! en Suisse – Halt! in der
Schweiz – Stop! in Switzerland
1937 CH Tempera 27,5 × 17,5 cm
Plakatentwurf – Poster design
Donation Schweiz Tourismus,
Zürich

78 Herbert Leupin (1916–1999)
Maryland/Stella Filtra
1956 CH Offset 127 × 90 cm

79 Donald Brun (1909–1999)
Pro Juventute
ca. 1955 CH Lithografie –
Lithograph 128 × 90,5 cm

80 Herbert Leupin (1916–1999)
Tat … sachen! – F … acts!
1963 CH Offset 128 × 90,5 cm

81 Niklaus Stoecklin (1896–1982)
Vim putzt alles – Vim Cleans
Everything
1926 CH Lithografie – Lithograph
127 × 90 cm

82 Michael Engelmann (1928–1966)
Roth-Händle/Naturrein – Roth-Händle/
Pure as Nature
1959 DE Offset 118,5 × 83,5 cm

83 Michael Engelmann (1928–1966)
Roth-Händle/Naturrein – Roth-Händle/
Pure as Nature
1963 DE Offset 128 × 90,5 cm

84 Lutz Peltzer (1925–2003)
Alfred Hitchcock's Psycho
1960 DE Offset 84,5 × 59,5 cm

85 Karel Vaca (1919–1989)
Promiň, že je to málo – Verzeih, dass
es so wenig ist – Sorry, It's Not Much
1984 CS Offset 84 × 60 cm

86 Hans Erni (1909–2015)
Rettet das Wasser – Save our Water
1961 CH Tiefdruck – Gravure print
128 × 90,5 cm

87 Otto Baumberger (1889–1961)
Les 650 ans de la Confédération/
Festival national à Schwytz – 650
Jahre Eidgenossenschaft/Nationalfeier
in Schwyz – 650 Years of the
Confederation/National Celebrations
in Schwyz
1941 CH Lithografie – Lithograph
128 × 91 cm

88 Shigeo Fukuda (1932–2009)
The Impact of the Holocaust and
Genocide on Jews & Christians/
Remembering for the Future/An Inter-
national Scholars' Conference –
Die Auswirkung des Holocaust und
Genozids an Juden & Christen/
Erinnern für die Zukunft/Eine inter-
nationale Schülerkonferenz
1988 GB Siebdruck – Screenprint
103 × 73 cm
Donation DNP Foundation for Cultural
Promotion, Tokio und Shizuko Fukuda

89 anonym
24 Avril/Journée de solidarité avec
la jeunesse et les étudiants en
lutte contre le colonialisme, pour
l'indépendance nationale et la
coexistence pacifique – 24. April/
Solidaritätstag mit der Jugend und
den Studenten im Kampf gegen den
Kolonialismus, für die nationale
Unabhängigkeit und das friedliche
Zusammenleben – Day of Solidarity
with Young People and Students
Fighting Against Colonialism, for
National Independence and Peaceful
Co-existence
1972 FR Offset 39,5 × 27,5 cm

90 Sandberg-Kollektiv
Zwischen Deutschen eine Mauer,
neue Trümmer, neue Trauer, neuen
Krieg will Adenauer! Fort mit ihm! –
Adenauer wants a wall between
Germans, more ruins, more grief,
another war! Away with him!
ca. 1960 DD Lithografie – Lithograph
83,5 × 59 cm

91 anonym
Frauenstimmrecht Nein/Basler
Frauenkomitee gegen das Frauenstimmrecht – Women's Right
to Vote No/Basel Committee against
Women's Suffrage
1959 CH Lithografie – Lithograph
127 × 90,5 cm

92 Sheldon-Claire Company
What's a Dollar Worth?/Produce
Better/Live Better – Wie viel ist ein
Dollar wert?/Produziere besser/
Lebe besser
1949 US Offset 92 × 61 cm

93 Theyre Lee-Elliott (1903–1988)
Four Times the Number Carried/
Up and Down – Viermal so viele
Fahrgäste/Auf und ab
1936 GB Lithografie – Lithograph
101 × 63 cm

94 Hans Aeschbach (1911–1999)
Sammlung Für das Alter –
Collection For the Elderly
1947 CH Gouache 127 × 90,5 cm
Plakatentwurf – Poster design
Donation Pro Senectute, Zürich

95 Ferdinand Maire (1901–1963)
Pensez à la vieillesse – Denkt an das
Alter – Remember the Elderly
ca. 1930 CH Gouache, Pastellkreide –
Gouache, chalk pastel 128,5 × 90,5 cm
Plakatentwurf – Poster design
Donation Pro Senectute, Zürich

96 Fridolin Müller (1926–2006)
Photo: Willi S. Eberle (1931–)
Für das Alter – For the Elderly
1964 CH Gouache, Fotografie –
Gouache, photography
128,5 × 90,5 cm
Plakatentwurf – Poster design
Donation Pro Senectute, Zürich

97 Karl Bickel (1886–1982)
Ja/Alter/Invalidität – Yes/
Old Age/Invalidity
1925 CH Lithografie – Lithograph
127 × 90 cm

98 Hans Rudolf Lauterburg (1924–)
Photo: Fernand Rausser (1926–)
Freiwillige Spende für das Alter –
Voluntary Donation for the Elderly
1963 CH Offset 128 × 90,5 cm

99 Koichi Satō (1944–)
Ongakuza/Seifenblasen schwebten,
sie schwebten in den Weltraum –
Ongakuza/Soap Bubbles Floated,
They Floated into Outer Space
1989 JP Offset 103 × 73 cm

100 Walter Käch (1901–1970)
Ausstellung des IV. Internationalen
Radiologenkongresses in
Zürich/Kunstgewerbemuseum –
Exhibition of the 4th International
Radiologists Congress in
Zurich/Kunstgewerbemuseum
1934 CH Lithografie – Lithograph
127 × 90 cm

101 Eric Andersen (1981–)
When we last met I should have
said marriage will be a disaster but
death might be a success. – Als
wir uns das letzte Mal trafen, hätte
ich sagen sollen, Heiraten wird ein
Desaster sein, aber der Tod könnte
ein Erfolg sein.
2013 CH Xerox 128 × 90,5 cm
Donation Eric Andersen

102 anonym
Útěk v řetězech – Flucht in Ketten –
The Defiant Ones
1960 CS Offset 41 × 28,5 cm
Donation Peter Leuenberger

103 M. Rojas
Pasaron los fascistas/… su huella –
Die Faschisten zogen vorbei …
ihre Spur – The Fascists passed by …
This is what they left
ca. 1937 ES Lithografie – Lithograph
100 × 70,5 cm

104 Piär Amrein (1957–)
Handmade
2005 CH Xerox 42 × 30 cm
Donation Piär Amrein

105 IBM Corporation, IBM Boulder
Design Center
Pam Woll
Equal Opportunity/IBM –
Chancengleichheit/IBM
1992 US Siebdruck – Screenprint
53,5 × 38 cm
Donation Graphis Verlag, Zürich

106 Pedro Yamashita (1947–)
No War/Don't Attack Iraq – Kein
Krieg/Keinen Angriff auf den Irak
2003 JP Siebdruck – Screenprint
119 × 84 cm
Donation Pedro Yamashita

107 Paul Brühwiler (1939–)
Plakate von Pabrü/Deutsches Plakat-
museum Essen – Pabrü Posters/
Deutsches Plakatmuseum Essen
2000 DE Offset 119 × 84 cm
Donation Paul Brühwiler

108 Cornel Windlin (1964–)
Act Now/Contribute to Parco's
«Visualize the Future» exhibition –
Handle jetzt/Trage zur Ausstellung
«Visualize the Future» bei
1992 JP Siebdruck – Screenprint
59,5 × 42 cm

109 Sabina Albanese (1977–)
Infotag/Hochschule Luzern/Design &
Kunst – Information Day/Luzern
University of Applied Sciences and
Arts/Design & Art
2008 CH Siebdruck – Screenprint
128,5 × 90 cm
Donation Sabina Albanese

110 Paul Brühwiler (1939–)
10 Jahre Filmpodium im «Studio 4» –
10 Years of Filmpodium at Studio 4
1993 CH Siebdruck – Screenprint
128 × 90,5 cm

111 Cornel Windlin (1964–)/
Gregor Huber (1978–)
Volpone/Schauspielhaus Zürich
2010 CH Siebdruck – Screenprint
128 × 90 cm
Donation Schauspielhaus Zürich

112 Bartle Bogle Hegarty
Mike Wells
Levis 511/Zip Fly
1995 GB Offset 44 × 29 cm
Donation Graphis Verlag, Zürich

113 Armin Hofmann (1920–)
Photo: Max Mathys (1933–)
Stadttheater Basel 63/64
1963 CH Offset 128 × 90,5 cm

Ausgewählte Literatur / Selected Bibliography

Barnett, Dene et al., «Gestik», in: *Historisches Wörterbuch der Rhetorik,* vol. 3, Darmstadt 1996, col. 972–989.

Boehm, Gottfried, Sebastian Egenhofer, Christian Spies (eds.), *Zeigen. Die Rhetorik des Sichtbaren*, München 2010.

Brun, Jean, *La main, essentiellement*, Paris 1998.

Fischer-Lichte, Erika, Christoph Wulf (eds.), *Gesten. Inszenierung, Aufführung, Praxis*, München 2010.

Gröning, Karl, *Hände berühren, begreifen, formen …*, München 2000.

Grosse, Julia, Judith Reker, *Versteh mich nicht falsch! Gesten weltweit*, München 2010.

Heiz, André Vladimir (ed.), *Grundlagen der Gestaltung*, Zürich 2012.

Leroi-Gourhan, André, *Hand und Wort. Die Evolution von Technik, Sprache und Kunst*, Frankfurt am Main 1980.

Lévy, Jean-Benoît, *Handbook*, Baden 2007.

Müller, Cornelia, «Eine kleine Kulturgeschichte der Gestenbetrachtung», in: *Psychotherapie und Sozialforschung 4* (1), 2002, p. 3–29.

Munari, Bruno, *Speak Italian: The Fine Art of the Gesture,* San Francisco 2005.

Napier, John, *Hands*, Princeton 1993.

Schneider Brakel, Franz (ed.), *Gesten: ein Buchprojekt von Fotografie-Studenten der Hochschule für Grafik und Buchkunst Leipzig*, Köln 1996.

Thaler, Kurt, *Zugreifen! Die Plakatsammlung des Museum für Gestaltung zu Gast bei der Schweizerischen Nationalbank 02*, exhibition brochure, Zürich 2001.

Wehr, Marco, Martin Weinmann, *Die Hand, Werkzeug des Geistes*, Heidelberg 1999.

Wilson, Frank R., *Die Hand – Geniestreich der Evolution*, Stuttgart 2000.

Wulf, Christoph, Birgit Althans, Kathrin Audehm et al., *Die Geste in Erziehung, Bildung und Sozialisation*, Wiesbaden 2011.

Autoren / Authors

Bettina Richter
Geboren 1964, Kunsthistorikerin. 1996 Dissertation über die Antikriegsgrafiken von Théophile-Alexandre Steinlen. 1997–2006 wissenschaftliche Mitarbeiterin in der Plakatsammlung des Museum für Gestaltung Zürich. Seit 2006 Kuratorin der Plakatsammlung. Nebenbei Tätigkeit als Dozentin an der Zürcher Hochschule der Künste sowie als freischaffende Autorin.

Born in 1964, art historian. 1996 dissertation on the antiwar graphics of Théophile-Alexandre Steinlen. From 1997 to 2006, served as a research associate in the Poster Collection of the Museum für Gestaltung Zürich, since 2006 as its curator. Also lectures at the Zürcher Hochschule der Künste and works as a freelance writer.

Arne Scheuermann
Kommunikationsdesigner und Designforscher. 2000–2005 unterrichtete er unter anderem Typografie, Entwicklung und Vermittlung experimenteller Filmformen und Theorie der Bildgestaltung an der Universität Wuppertal. Promotion 2007 zur Theorie des Filmemachens am Beispiel von Affekten in Action-Adventure-Filmen. Seit 2005 Leiter des Forschungsschwerpunkts Kommunikationsdesign an der Hochschule der Künste Bern HKB und dort auch Professor für Designtheorie. Er forscht vor allem zur visuellen Rhetorik und ihrer Geschichte sowie zu angewandten Fragen rund um Grafikdesign im Gesundheitswesen. Publikationen unter anderem mit Gesche Joost, *Design als Rhetorik*, Basel 2008; *Zur Theorie des Filmemachens*, München 2009; mit Francesca Vidal, *Handbuch Medienrhetorik*, Berlin/Boston 2016. Seit 2014 Präsident des Swiss Design Network SDN.

Communication designer and design researcher. From 2000 to 2005 Arne Scheuermann taught at the University of Wuppertal, where his subjects included typography, the development and communication of experimental forms of film and the theory of image design. In 2007 he earned a doctorate in the theory of filmmaking with a dissertation that explored examples of affect in action and adventure films. Since 2005 he has been the head of the research focus area "Communication Design" at the Bern University of Arts (BUA), where he is also professor of design theory. His research focuses primarily on visual rhetoric and its history, as well as on applied aspects of graphic design in the health care sector. His publications include *Design als Rhetorik*, ed. with Gesche Joost, Basel 2009; *Zur Theorie des Filmemachens*, Munich, 2009; and *Handbuch Medienrhetorik*, ed. with Francesca Vidal, Berlin/Boston, 2016. Since 2014 he has been president of the Swiss Design Network (SDN).

Dank / Acknowledgments

Publikations- und Ausstellungsprojekte sind immer
ein willkommener Anlass, den eigenen, umfangreichen
Bestand an Plakaten themenspezifisch zu sichten, aufzu-
arbeiten und zu ergänzen. Für die vorliegende Publikation
konnten wir auf viele Plakatklassiker zurückgreifen, die
der Sammlung im Verlauf ihrer Geschichte als Donation
übergeben wurden. Zudem haben wir aktuelle Plakate
zeitgenössischer Gestalterinnen und Gestalter erhalten.
Für das uns geschenkte Vertrauen ebenso wie für Anre-
gungen und Informationen zum Thema möchten wir uns
an dieser Stelle ganz herzlich bedanken.

Publication and exhibition projects are always welcome
occasions to examine and work with our own extensive
holdings of posters with a specific theme in mind,
and also to update it with targeted acquisitions. For this
publication we were able to draw on numerous classic
posters that have been donated to the collection over the
course of its history. In addition, we have received posters
from contemporary designers. We would like to use this
opportunity to express our sincere thanks for the trust
placed in us and for the suggestions and information on
the topic.

Museum für Gestaltung Zürich

Eine Publikation des Museum für Gestaltung Zürich
Christian Brändle, Direktor

A Publication of the Museum für Gestaltung Zürich
Christian Brändle, Director

Die Hand / The Hand
Konzept und Redaktion / Concept and editing:
Mirjam Fischer, Christina Reble, Bettina Richter
Gestaltung / Design: Integral Lars Müller
Übersetzung / Translation (Ger.–Eng.): Chris Walton (Essay),
Helen Ferguson (Vorwort / Foreword)
Lektorat Deutsch / German copyediting: Markus Zehentbauer
Lektorat Englisch / English copyediting: Adam Blauhut
Lithografie / Repro: Ast & Fischer AG, Wabern
Druck, Einband / Printing, binding: Kösel, Altusried-Krugzell,
Germany

Reihe / «Poster Collection» Series
Herausgegeben von / Edited by
Museum für Gestaltung Zürich, Plakatsammlung
Bettina Richter, Kuratorin der Plakatsammlung /
Curator of the Poster Collection
In Zusammenarbeit mit / In cooperation with
Mirjam Fischer, Publikationen / Publications,
Museum für Gestaltung Zürich

© 2015
Zürcher Hochschule der Künste, Zürcher Fachhochschule
und Lars Müller Publishers

Z — hdk

Zürcher Hochschule der Künste
Zurich University of the Arts

Museum für Gestaltung Zürich – Schaudepot
Pfingstweidstrasse 96
CH-8005 Zürich / Switzerland
www.museum-gestaltung.ch
www.eMuseum.ch

Museum für Gestaltung Zürich
Plakatsammlung / Poster Collection
CH-8005 Zürich / Switzerland
sammlungen@museum-gestaltung.ch

Lars Müller Publishers
CH-8005 Zürich / Switzerland
books@lars-muller.ch
www.lars-mueller-publishers.com

ISBN 978-3-03778-477-8
Erste Auflage / First Edition

Printed in Germany

Wir danken für Unterstützung /
For their support we wish to thank:

.:: APG|SGA

POSTER COLLECTION

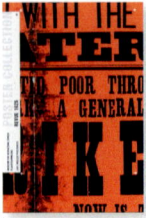
01 REVUE 1926

02 DONALD BRUN

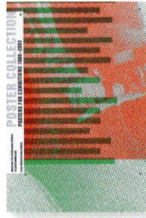
03 POSTERS FOR EXHIBITIONS 1980–2000

04 HORS-SOL

05 TYPOTECTURE

06 VISUAL STRATEGIES AGAINST AIDS

07 ARMIN HOFMANN

08 BLACK AND WHITE

09 RALPH SCHRAIVOGEL

10 MICHAEL ENGELMANN

11 HANDMADE

12 CATHERINE ZASK

13 TYPO CHINA

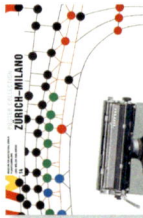
14 ZÜRICH–MILANO

15 BREAKING THE RULES

16 COMIX!

17 PHOTO GRAPHICS

18 OTTO BAUMBERGER

19 HEAD TO HEAD

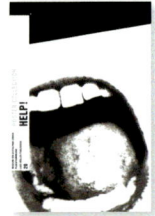
20 HELP!

21 PARADISE SWITZERLAND

22 LETTERS ONLY

23 IN SERIES

24 THE MAGIC OF THINGS

25 JOSEF MÜLLER-BROCKMANN

26 JAPAN–NIPPON